decorating GLASS

* PAINTING
* EMBOSSING
* ENGRAVING
* ETCHING

Polly Rothenberg

CROWN PUBLISHERS, INC., NEW YORK

Also by the Author

THE COMPLETE BOOK OF CERAMIC ART
THE COMPLETE BOOK OF CREATIVE GLASS ART
CREATIVE STAINED GLASS
METAL ENAMELING

First published January 1977

Inquiries should be addressed to Crown Publishers, Inc.,
One Park Avenue, New York, N.Y. 10016.

Printed in the United States of America
Published simultaneously in Canada by
General Publishing Company Limited
Design: Deborah Daly

Library of Congress Cataloging in Publication Data

Rothenberg, Polly.
    Decorating glass—painting, embossing, engraving.
etching.

    Includes index.
    1. Glass craft.   I.   Title.
TT298.R68 1976   748.6   76-18967
ISBN 0-517-52391-4
ISBN 0-517-52392-2 pbk.

*Contents

Painted view of Nürnberg, Germany, on a blown glass covered cup with three blown feet. Dated 1665. Photograph by courtesy of *The Toledo Museum of Art. Gift of Edward Drummond Libbey.*

1
* Introduction

The charm and beauty of color and pattern on your own personally ornamented glass can brighten your home and provide hours of creative enjoyment. It is not necessary to have an extensive art education to be able to decorate glass. Anyone who loves beauty and who has the patience to pursue it can follow the simple but precise directions in this book. To guide your way, detailed descriptions of techniques and materials are presented with each process described here, such as unfired and fired painting, gilding, embossing, etching, and others. Illustrated step-by-step instructions are simple and easy to follow. Beginning with basic projects, each technique progresses to more complex examples that may include two or more of the processes.

Both sheet glass and preformed three-dimensional glassware are suitable for hand decoration. Clear window glass in single and double strengths, cathedral, antique, and flashed stained glass are employed for sheet projects in this book. Well-formed three-dimensional articles in clear and colored glass with plain surface areas suitable for hand decoration are found at auctions, art department clearances, secondhand shops, and in your own cupboards. Many of the objects shown in the illustrated projects were discovered in just such places.

The most exciting way to decorate glass is to combine a variety of methods to achieve the effect you desire. Beginning with your first projects, you will be delighted to find that you can create decorative glass medallions, panels, small windows, containers in opaque white or blue glass, bottles, clear or tinted glass tableware, and canisters that become lovely gifts or colorful accessories to enrich your life.

Eastern Bluebird and Mallard Duck painted in natural colors on clear glass with leaded borders. *Courtesy of Glass Masters Guild of New York.*

Snuff bottle with an underglass painting inside the bottle. Stopper is ruby glass with gold filigree setting. *From the collection of Wilma Cymbala.*

Painted glassware. Unfired paint in bright colors, by Wilma Cymbala.

Cutting Glass

You may want to cut the sheet glass you plan to decorate or to cut glass shapes for bonding embossed designs; in either case, you will find that cutting glass is essentially very simple if you follow certain precise directions. When glass is scored with the tiny sharp metal wheel set into one end of a metal or wooden-handled glass cutter, only the surface of the glass is fractured. The cut causes glass molecules to separate along the scored line *when adequate pressure is applied.* The pressure must be applied at once, if you would make a clean separation of the glass. If more than a couple of minutes elapse, the separated molecules of glass will partially heal so that a clean separation is not achieved, even though the scored line is still visible.

Certain safety precautions must be followed when you work with glass. If you see a choice piece partially buried beneath other glass, remove the upper pieces, starting from the top of the pile. If you try to shuffle them around with your bare hands, you are likely to receive multiple gashes. Wear gloves when you transport large glass sheets. To remove the sharp slivers that often appear along a freshly cut glass edge, scrape the edge with another piece of glass, or sand them under water. Avoid pressing your bare hands against the cutting surface after a session of glass cutting. The minute glass shards that litter the tabletop can cause small but painful cuts. Happily, very few glass craftsmen cut themselves severely.

The cutting table must be firm, flat, and level. To maintain good arm leverage it is best to stand while you cut glass. About 34 to 36 inches from the floor is adequate worktable height for the average person. Short pile carpet, a layer of sheet cork, or several sheets of paper make good cutting surfaces for the tabletop. Although a ruler can guide the cutter when straight lines are scored, it may have the annoying propensity of shifting suddenly or sliding on the glass just as you start to score. You can control this slippage by gluing a long, very thin strip of rubber to the underside of the straightedge. "Rug grip" sold in carpet stores is excellent for this purpose.

A glass cutter with a hard steel cutting wheel is adequate for general use and it will give long service when it is cared for properly. When not in use, the cutter should be stored in a bottle with enough kerosene or light oil to cover the wheel set in the end of the cutter. These glass cutters are sold in most hardware stores and they are very inexpensive.

Before cutting begins, clean the glass with detergent water to remove all soil that may cause the cutter to skip and make separation of the scored glass difficult or ragged. Lubricate the cutting wheel with kerosene before you start to score. Hold the cutter perpendicular to the tabletop when you score the glass. It can lean slightly toward you, but if it tilts sideways, one edge of the score line may be undercut and make a rough separation of the glass.

To begin, position the glass on the table, smoothest side up if it is stained glass. Dip the cutter into kerosene and dab it on a paper towel to remove excess oil. Hold the cutter as shown in the illustrations. To make a straight cut, begin about 1/16" from the edge of the glass to avoid chipping it and make a firm continuous even stroke with the cutter from one edge of the glass to the other *without pausing or lifting* the cutter. Score either toward you or away from you, whichever is easier and allows you to see where you are going. The cutter must not wander away from the line you are scoring. Press it firmly against the glass. It should make a soft steady scratching sound as it bites into the glass. Scoring the glass requires concentration. If the cutter begins to lean sideways, the cutting wheel may curve away from its designated line. Only experience can teach you how firmly to apply pressure. As you reach the opposite edge of the glass, relax your hand so you do not chip the glass.

As soon as the glass has been scored, lay one end of your cutter under the near end of the scored line and immediately press down firmly with your thumbs on each side of the line at the end nearest you. The scored glass should separate evenly. If it does not, lay the glass over the table edge so the scored line comes just beyond and parallel to the tabletop. With one hand spread out and pressing the glass firmly against the top of the table, snap the glass in two with the other hand, bending it down and away from the table. After these two efforts, if you have not separated the glass, hold it in one hand and with the cutter in the other hand tap firmly but gently all along the scored line from *underneath* the glass. Tap sharply from one end of the score line to the other. You should see a fracture developing along the line. Apply equal pressure to the two sides of the fracture line and snap the glass apart. Long curved lines are cut in the same way if they are not too sharply curved.

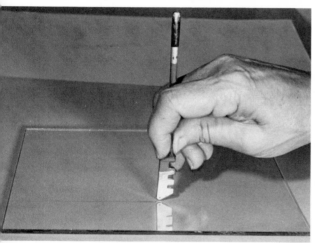

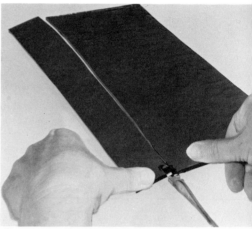

Hold the cutter perpendicular between first and second fingers. The thumb supports the cutter on the underside of the flat surface just above the cutter notches. The tiny cutting wheel rides on the glass.

As soon as the glass has been scored, lay one end of the cutter under the near end of the score line and immediately press firmly down on each side of the line. The glass should separate easily.

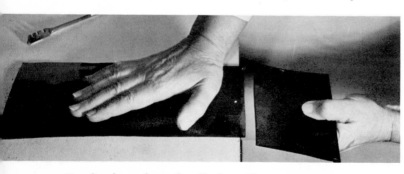

Another method of separating the glass. With one hand pressing the glass against the tabletop, and with the score line extending over the edge and parallel to it, snap the glass down and out.

Tap firmly and gently all along the scored line underneath the glass for another way to separate it. You will see a fracture developing under the scored line. Snap the glass down and outward with your hands.

Small shapes are scored and snapped apart on the score line with the thumbs and curled forefingers pressing down and outward.

To cut shaped glass pieces, make an exact stiff paper template pattern of the shape you will cut. Lay it on a clean piece of glass with at least 3/4" margin all around the template. With the fingers of one hand spread out on the template, hold it firmly against the glass, taking care that it does not slip while you are scoring around it. One side of the glass shape is scored and separated at a time. Dip the cutter into kerosene and dab it on a paper towel. Begin at one edge of the glass and score along one side of the pattern, continuing beyond it to the other edge without lifting the cutter. Lay down the cutter at once and pick up the glass before the score line heals as described earlier. Apply firm equal pressure on each side of the scored line, and snap the glass down and out. If you are cutting off a thin strip of glass, grasp it on the narrow side of the score line with flat end pliers or glass pliers and on the other side with your other hand. It may be necessary to tap sharply along the underside of the score line to start the fracture. Press down and out on each side of the fracture line as described for straight cuts. If you try to complete the glass separation only by tapping it until it falls apart, you will have a ragged cut. Each side of the shape is cut by scoring and separating the same way, before the next side is scored.

When you have cut out the curved glass shape as best you can, you will probably be left with unwanted small projections along its edges. To pinch off small irregularities, use small straight-edged nippers to grasp only the portion you want to remove from the glass edge, and squeeze or pinch it with quick firm pressure until you literally bite off the glass protrusion with the nipper jaws. If you are cutting stained glass, you may occasionally encounter bubbles or other irregularities; ease the cutter over them gently without lifting it from the glass. These bubbles give beauty and character to the glass. With experience you will ride the cutter smoothly over them.

A circle cutter is required for cutting out perfect glass circles; or you can have them cut by your local glass supplier where you purchase the glass. To cut your own, follow exactly the instructions that accompany the

Glass shapes are cut out around small templates, one side at a time, with the cutter scoring from edge to edge of the glass.

To separate a thin glass strip from a wider strip, grasp the glass on the narrow side with pliers and on the other side with your hand. Notice that the glass is always held between thumb and curled forefinger to provide safe leverage for parting the glass.

Corners and unwanted projections are "grozed," or nipped off, with small flat-nosed pliers or grozing pliers.

circle cutter. If the cutter's rubber disk, which clamps it against the glass, tends to release the glass while you are cutting it, wipe the disk with a film of water, then clamp it down again. You should have no further difficulty with it. Glass cutting is fundamentally simple. Regardless of how awkward you may feel initially, do not become discouraged. Read the cutting instructions over several times until you feel ready to begin the fascinating experience of cutting glass.

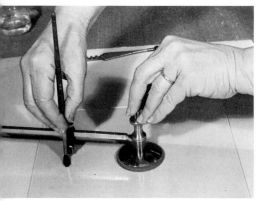 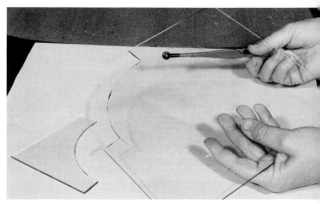

To cut circles, lift the cutting wheel and swinging arm of the cutter off the glass while you hold a kerosened brush against the cutter. Scribe a full circle with the brush (not with the cutting wheel) to put kerosene where the cutter will score the glass. Put down the brush, press the cutting wheel against the glass, and score it on the kerosened path made by the brush.

If the glass has not separated, light tapping under the scored lines should complete the separation.

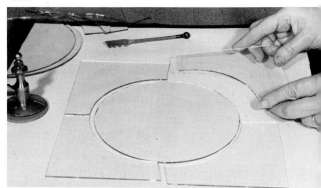

When the glass circle is separated, sand the edges lightly with wet carborundum paper.

A FULL-RIGGED SHIP. Glass Masters Guild. Reproduction of sixteenth-century scenes. Triptych glass painted in colors.

2

* Painting Glass

Unfired Paints

One of the most appealing methods of decorating glass today is the art of painting it in beautiful colors that do not need to be fired in a kiln. Unlike porous painted surfaces, glass is completely nonabsorbent. Paint that will not be fired is "flowed on" rather than brushed in, an entirely different process from painting on canvas, wood, paper, or other porous materials. Brushstrokes are delicate, but well defined. Glimpses of clear glass may be left visible within the painted patterns to provide tiny transparent highlights that preserve its natural charm. Whatever painted design is applied to one side of a three-dimensional transparent form may

A SUN FACE. *(Left)* Detail from King's College Chapel at Cambridge (1540). Painted on light blue stained glass. Leaded frame.

THE SUN, MOON, AND STAR. *(Right)* Roundel painted in bright colors. Adapted from seventeenth-century engraving. Leaded frame. *Both by courtesy of Glass Masters Guild of New York.*

be seen through it and become a part of the overall effect on the opposite side of the piece.

The beauty of painted glass decoration depends upon the neatness of the executed design. Because it is difficult to achieve a skillful correction on freshly painted glass, only a very simple initial project should be attempted by the beginner to lessen the probability of mistakes. It is advisable to paint on flat sheet window glass or stained glass until you become accustomed to the "feel" of painting on this hard glossy material before you progress to curved surfaces. A first project on flat glass may indeed be quite attractive. Beautiful medallions are created on flat glass circles, rectangles, and even on free-form flat shapes.

PREPARING THE GLASS AND DESIGN

The initial step is to cut a rectangle of single-strength window glass about 6½" by 8". If you should have small mullioned windows, a glass that fits within one of the mullioned frames might be a choice to consider. When you have cut the glass, for safety's sake sand the cut edges under water with fine-grained *wettable* type carborundum paper, which will remove sharp edges without unduly roughening them. The next step is very important. Glass that will be painted must be *absolutely clean.* Paint will not adhere well to damp, soiled, or oily glass. Wipe it with turpentine or paint thinner if it seems sticky or very soiled. Then wash it in warm detergent water, rinse it, and dry it. Take care to hold the glass by its edges to keep it clean.

When the glass has been prepared, trace around your glass rectangle on drawing paper. Carefully draw a simple line design within the outlines of the glass rectangle, and retrace all the design lines with a fine-pointed, black felt-tipped marker, or pen and ink, to make them dark enough to be seen through the glass. If you use a medium or dark stained glass, you may not be able to see the lines. When you have retraced your design, position the clean glass on top of it so the edges fit the traced outline you drew around the glass. Hold it firmly in position while you tape the glass edges to the drawing paper. Then set it aside while you prepare your work area and materials.

WORK AREA AND MATERIALS

The worktable surface can be covered with a sheet of white vinyl plastic, the kind that is sold by the yard for tablecloths. A plain white oilcloth will serve equally well. Turn under the edges and tack them under the table edge. Stack some newssheets and paper towels nearby to protect the table cover when you use paints, turpentine, soiled rags, wet brushes, and other materials as you may need them.

An inexpensive piece of equipment that is very useful when you paint glass, although not absolutely essential, is an *armrest*, or "bridge," formed from a board with flat wood blocks nailed underneath each end. It will elevate your hand and wrist above the flat glass surface while you paint. It will prevent them from soiling the glass or smearing a freshly painted design while you work. The glass and the paper pattern that are taped together are rotated on top of the worktable as the painting progresses. Your brush is applied in the direction easiest for you to control. The heel of your hand rests on the bridge while wrist and finger action manipulate the brush. This is a very different method from painting on canvas. If you do not use a bridge for glass painting, the glass must still be protected from finger marks. A box of tissues at hand is very convenient.

BRUSHES

Fine-pointed *sable brushes* in very small sizes: #0, #1, a #1 sable liner with long flexible bristles for painting the necessary fine lines around curves, and a #3 or #4 pointed sable brush for fill-in areas are adequate for the beginner. When you use several colors, it is convenient to have extra small brushes at hand. As experience is gained in glass painting, you will discover whether you need additional brushes. If you take care of them, they will last a long time. Whenever you finish a session of painting, wipe all excess paint from the brushes with paper towels or rags, clean them with turpentine or paint thinner, and wash them with mild soap and warm water. After you have rinsed them thoroughly, shape the round brush points and flatten the square ones with your fingers. Put them away in a covered box when they are dry.

PAINTS

Unfired paints employed on projects in this book are regular glass stains for applying transparent colors, and artist's tube oil paints mixed with *spar* varnish and a few drops of turpentine are for painting both transparents and opaques. A medicine dropper is a wonderful convenience for adding drops of turpentine to oil paint mixtures. Spar varnish gives water resistance to oil paints if they are allowed to dry for about two weeks after the painting is completed, before they are handled. Artist's oil paints come in many lovely hues and the tubes are easy to store. Their caps will not stick if you wipe any particles of paint from the threads of the tubes before you replace their caps. However, if a cap should stick stubbornly, do not force it; hold the cap end of the tube under hot water for a few moments and the cap should come off easily. The tube paints are mixed with the varnish in very small amounts as they are needed. Don't forget the turpentine!

Always keep a *varnish* can lid closed when you are not actually using the varnish. When varnish is exposed to the air, the spirits begin to evaporate, causing the varnish to thicken and form a surface "skin." Varnish should not be shaken or stirred; the resultant bubbles may pit the surface of your painting. By keeping the varnish can and lid wiped clean with a damp turpentined rag, the lid will fit tightly and is less likely to stick shut. If a thick wrinkled skin forms over the top of the varnish in a partly full can, you may be able to salvage the varnish by cutting cleanly around the edge of the skin and lifting it off with the knife. If a can is opened frequently, it will form a skin regardless of how tightly it is closed betweentimes. When varnish thickens and becomes jellylike, the best advice is to discard it and obtain a fresh unopened can. It is wise to buy the smallest size can available. A good brush for blending the small amounts of tube oil paint and varnish that should be mixed at one time is a #4 square-tipped shader. If you use a flat piece of glass for a palette, the paint can be blended with a palette knife. A blending brush should not be used for painting.

When the glass and work area are prepared and the materials are assembled, it is time to mix the paint for your project. Blend a small amount of artist's tube oil paint (about 1/8" from the tube) with three parts spar varnish. Three drops of turpentine are added with the medicine dropper. This mixture should be adequate for the fine outlining. Equal parts paint to varnish give a good opaque mixture, but this requires a longer drying time. The first paint mixture, which is stronger in varnish, will outline the design and dry quickly to serve as a small "fence" that will hold the fill-in color from spreading over the nonabsorbent glass.

A fine-pointed soft sable brush, #1 or #0, is rolled in the paint mixture. Touch it lightly to a palette to relieve its tip of excess paint. With the tip of the brush, carefully trace a thin outline onto the glass over the design outline on the drawing beneath it. Let the paint dry for about an hour. When the painted lines have set, a clean brush is rolled in the fill-in color. If the brush tends to drip paint, touch its tip lightly to your palette. With the brush nearly perpendicular, apply it gently to the glass within the painted outline and let some of the paint flow off the end of the brush tip. Lift the brush and touch the tip to the glass again. You will soon be able to brush it lightly along on the glass, letting the paint flow as you move the tip over the glass. Keep the brush fairly full of paint *but not dripping.* If the paint tends to thicken, add a drop or two of turpentine. Dip the brush into a small container of turpentine from time to time and whisk it on a paper towel to keep it clean and flexible. For multicolor projects, each color is applied and allowed to set before the next color is applied. Then hold the glass up to the light and see whether you want to add a second thin layer to any uneven color. Highlights and shadows or other finishing details can be added just as on any other kind of painting. Let the paint dry ten days or longer before the glass is handled.

If you plan to use *transparent* tube oil paint, follow the same directions as those given for opaque oils. Transparent tube oil paint gives a rich effect on a three-dimensional glass subject, especially when combined with gold or silver metallic paint. Unfired painted glass can be washed gently in warm water, then dried. Of course you wouldn't run the glass through a dishwasher. With care, glass colors blended from oil paint, spar varnish, and turpentine can remain bright indefinitely.

The following three projects demonstrate different types of painting on small glass rectangles.

PROJECTS

Silhouette on Clear Glass

Before beginning a painted glass project, read again the directions under "Unfired Paints." The initial demonstration is a silhouette painting on a rectangle of single-strength window glass, 6½" by 7½". Black tube oil paint (about 1/8"), spar varnish, and a few drops of turpentine are blended thoroughly in a small container or on a glass palette. It is essential to add the few drops of turpentine to the paint; otherwise it will not set or dry for several days. The brush for outlining this first design on glass is a #1 sable liner. Its bristles are long, thin, and flexible. When the outline design has been drawn on paper and retraced with a felt-tipped marker, it is taped beneath the glass. A margin of paper extending around the glass can be held and manipulated to rotate the project as painting progresses. Very thin lines are traced on the clean glass, over the lines beneath it. The glass is set aside to dry when the outlining is completed. The dry painted outline will serve as a little "fence" to keep the fill-in paint from spreading in an uncontrolled manner. Remember, glass is completely nonabsorbent; paint cannot be brushed in as is done on other types of material.

The brush for the second step in this project is a #3 sable liner. The outlines are filled in as detailed in the general directions for unfired paints. When the first painted coat is completed, the glass is dried overnight. A second coat of black paint mixture is applied thinly and dried for

Line sketch to fit within the outline of the glass panel.

a smooth opaque silhouette. A one-color painting can be set in a transparent plastic easel, or it can be framed against a contrasting background for a rich effect. If you plan to frame a glass painting, obtain the frame before the glass is cut. Some frames can be bought with glass already in them. Although picture glass is thin, with care it can be utilized for a glass painting. The painted glass can be turned over and framed with the painted side reversed. It will give subtle depth to the picture. (See "Reverse Painting Under Glass.")

The lines are emphasized with a felt-tipped marker.

The clean glass is positioned on top the design and taped to the paper beneath it. Hands are supported on a wood "bridge." With the tip of a #1 sable liner brush, thin lines are traced onto the glass over the drawn lines beneath it. Keep the brush clean with turpentine. Let the painted lines set.

The glass is propped up at one end so cast shadows do not obscure the paint outlines as you fill them in with a #3 liner. When the first coat of paint is dry, apply a second coat.

Interesting details complete the composition. Clear glass highlights have been left within painted areas.

SHEPHERD WITH DRUM AND SHEPHERD WITH PIPE. Glass Masters Guild. Amber and blue painting on pale tan seedy glass. 7⅜ inches high. Adapted from Book of Hours (sixteenth century.)

One-Color Door Panels

The imaginative potential of ordinary clear window glass as a base for painting makes possible inexpensive but charming decorative glass projects. Four identical glass rectangles are cut and painted to suit small window openings in a door. This is not a difficult project, but thin lines and precise execution are important for this formal pattern.

The usual full-size outlined drawing (or cartoon) is made and retraced with a felt-tipped marker. It is taped beneath the first of the four window-panes. A very small amount of black tube oil paint, about 1/8", is *blended* with an equal amount of spar varnish and a few drops of turpentine. The #1 red sable liner is rolled in the paint to work plenty of pigment into the bristles; then it is stroked on a palette to shape it into a point for making the very thin outlines of the design. It must retain enough paint to flow smoothly through a complete stroke without suddenly going dry. All the design is outlined except the crosshatched center square which is painted just as it appears. To keep a brush clean of accumulated paint, dip it into turpentine from time to time and whisk it on paper toweling. As soon as the lines have set, the first fill-in coat is applied with a #3 liner. It is dried, and a second coat is added to cover any thin areas. The glass is left to dry overnight. Any ragged spots that show up can be carved away with a single-edged razor blade after the final coat has set for at least 24 hours. The three additional panes are painted and dried to match the first one. They are all installed against existing window glass with thin strips of wood, painted to match the door. These very thin, even wood strips were obtained from a model airplane hobby store which stocks all sizes of thin narrow wood strips and tiny tacks suitable for installing the strips into the window frames against the side edges of each glass. The wood strips make a much neater finish around these small panes than putty would offer. For this project, light-colored stained glass can be substituted for window glass to provide a rich effect.

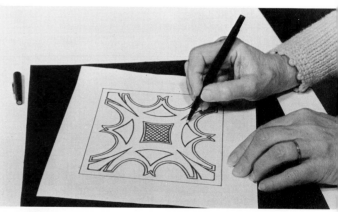

Full-size outline sketch is re-traced with a fine-pointed felt-tip marker.

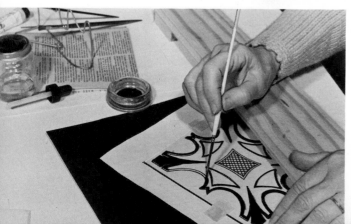

The drawing is taped beneath single-strength window glass. Hands are supported on a bridge. The outlines are filled in with a small liner brush.

When the paint is completely dry, any ragged spots are carved away with a single-edged razor blade.

Four matching panes are installed against existing window glass. Notice how the design carries from glass to glass with a "broken circle" effect.

Multicolor Paints on Stained Glass

The demonstrated stained-glass project is painted in several unfired opaque colors. Transparent paints would appear grayed by light transmitted through the colored glass. A design sketch is emphasized with a fine-pointed felt marker and it is taped beneath the rectangle of amber yellow stained glass. Since a gilt border is planned for this glass picture, a suitable border is outlined on a separate paper and set aside temporarily while a very small amount of green oil paint mixture for outlining the design edges is blended with varnish and turpentine. Fine green lines are

Whimsical storybook characters. Adapted and painted by John Nussbaum and Jean Holly Clark for Glass Masters Guild.

traced on the glass over the pattern beneath it with a #0 pointed brush. When the paint has set, fill-in colors are applied with #1 and #3 brushes, one color at a time; each is allowed to set before the next color is applied. Colors are: green stems and leaves, pink clover blossoms, and light blue with dark borders and spots for butterfly wings. The glass is left to dry overnight. When the paint is no longer sticky, the glass is taped over the separate border drawing and gilded with Liquid Leaf. Thin outlines are not required here because the gilt sets very quickly and does not need to be confined with painted outlines. (For Liquid Leaf see "Supply Sources.")

The stained glass edges are taped with narrow adhesive-backed copper tape. The glass picture is displayed on a plastic easel bought in a picture-framing store. It is effective for supporting glass because the easel is practically invisible behind it.

An outline sketch is retraced with a felt-tip marker.

A suitable border is outlined on a separate paper.

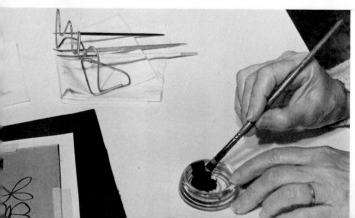

Artist's tube oil paint, varnish, and a few drops of turpentine are blended with a square-tipped shader used only for mixing the paint. Notice the handy brush holder, constructed from a wire coat hanger, for supporting wet paint brushes.

Fine green lines are traced on light yellow seedy stained glass.

Colors are applied with #1 and #3 brushes, one color at a time. Each color is allowed to set before the next color is applied. Two or three drops of turpentine in the paint and varnish mixture will set the colors in an hour or two. Thin gold-line accents are added with Liquid Leaf.

When the colors have dried overnight and are no longer sticky, the glass is taped over the separate border drawing. Unfired Liquid Leaf is traced over the border design.

The stained glass edges are bound with narrow adhesive-backed copper tape.

Metallic Paints, Unfired

Delicate gold and silver accents and lines bring glamour and beauty to any decorative glass method. They add distinction to even plain forms by collecting and dispersing pinpoints of gleaming metallic rays of light. Transmitted light will only silhouette the gilt because it is opaque; but reflected light on gold edges or surface patterns bestows on them the rich gleam of precious metal. Some metallic lusters do not require firing.

These metallic paints are applied to glass projects that will not be subjected to the heat of the kiln. Projects that will be fired to 1100°F or higher can be gilded with fired metallic paint. However, if you want a fired metallic rim or handle on a vessel that will be decorated with *unfired* colors or bonded with embossed glass, remember to apply and fire the gilt before any other ornamentation is added. Some vessels are handled frequently and unfired gold on a rim or handle can easily wear off.

A delightful gilding product that does not require firing is available in some large art supply stores or directly from the manufacturer. It is Liquid Leaf. In addition to several exciting golds, it includes silver, pewter, copper, and brass colors. Liquid Leaf is not a heavy-duty product. It is intended for decorative purposes rather than for functional glass that might be rubbed or handled frequently. However, its durability can be extended with a sealer developed by the same manufacturer.

The glass surface that will be painted must be absolutely clean and free of oil from the fingers. Wash it in detergent water, rinse it in warm water, and dry it well. A brush suitable for application of metallic paints should not be used for any other purposes. Small flat or pointed sable brushes that do not shed hairs are fine for applying gilt. Loose hairs from a brush will leave annoying rough spots in the paint. The brush can be cleaned in a special product called Xylene or with lacquer thinner. To gild flat glass, tape the drawing underneath the glass so the two can be pivoted together as needed to reach all sides of the design. The guiding sketch can be taped inside a three-dimensional object.

Before you apply gilt, shake the bottle well and tape it to the table, or anchor it in a broader container to keep it from tipping over when the brush is dipped in it. These small bottles are easily tipped and all the expensive gilt may be lost. Apply the metallic paint as smoothly and carefully as possible. The luster dries rapidly, so avoid brushing over it. To do so will roughen it. After four hours, a second coat can be applied if necessary for a smooth coat. If you apply the second coat too soon, it may loosen the first coat. To gild a band around a lid or container, anchor it to a banding wheel with small lumps of modeling clay as illustrated. Revolve the wheel with one hand while the other hand applies the brush with special care. Brace the hand that holds the brush so it stays motionless. Very small brushes, #00, #0, and #1 will make delicate gilt accent lines along the edges of colored painted designs for a charming finish.

Transparent Glass Stains, Unfired

Glass stain colors are deep and rich; but glass stain is not a durable paint. It is intended for decorative projects only, and it is not practical for functional glassware. However, exciting glass paintings are possible with this material. It can be combined with other decorating methods where durability may not be essential. Glass stain is available only in transparent colors.

Glass stains are premixed in their small jars when you buy them. A paint thinner, available where the stains are sold, will thin them to make the deep colors lighter if you prefer. The stain is volatile and it evaporates rapidly. It may thicken on the brush after you have been painting with it for a while. When this occurs, dip the brush into a small container of thinner (a ketchup bottle lid holds enough), and wipe it on a paper towel to soften it and keep the stain flowing smoothly and the brush moving freely. Errors made with this paint are difficult to correct. But with practice, delightful results are possible.

The demonstrated window panel's marine design begins with a colorful exotic fish in vibrant orange, purple, and black. A line design is drawn to scale and size. It is anchored under the glass panel on the worktable. The painting is done freely on the glass surface with soft flat brushes, 1" or less in size. The fish is painted first on the demonstration panel, with each color applied separately, and left to dry a few hours before the next color is applied. The colored "stones" banked along the base of the composition are tiny glass jewels cut and fired to round their corners (at about 1350°–1400°F). They were cut from stained-glass scraps, saved from earlier projects. A line drawn across the lower part of the sketch under the glass panel guides the top limit of their application. Epoxy cement is applied and the glass stones are positioned one by one. Colors repeat the colors of the painting. A few little glass pieces are glued to the glass near the top of the panel to suggest small sea organisms and to catch stray beams of light. The panel is left to dry for a day or two, then it is *turned over.*

The back of this panel is painted freely with marine colors over the entire area with the exception of the space occupied by the fish design. It is left free of background paint so the colors of the fish remain bright and are not grayed by the blues and greens of the water's color. The area back of the colorful glass "stones" is painted in light chartreuse which blends with the colors of the stained glass bits and makes a sand-colored sea floor. After the paint has dried for several days, it is covered with spar varnish for more durability. When the varnish is dry, the panel is installed against a small windowpane.

Outlines of the fish are brushed on the glass above a drawn design sketch beneath it.

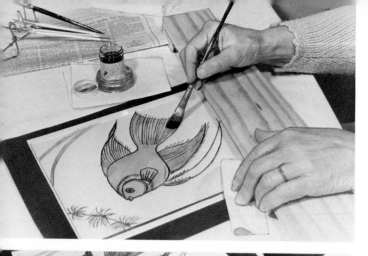

With a 1/2" soft flat water-color brush, the fish is painted freely in transparent glass stain. Colors are orange, purple, and black. *(See color plate.)* Each color is dried *before* the next color is applied.

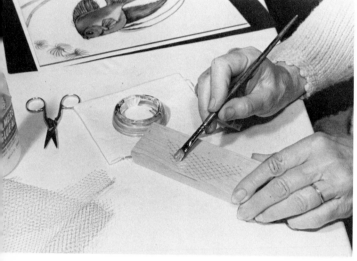

A piece of nylon netting is glued to a board and dabbed with white paint mixture that will be pressed lightly on the fish to make a pattern of dots.

The wet paint has collected on the knots in the mesh and it makes a rhythmical pattern of white multisized dots on the fish when the wood is pressed lightly against the *dried* bright paint.

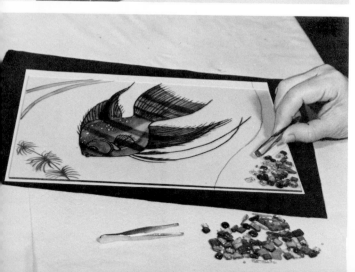

A line drawn across the lower part of the sketch under the glass panel guides the top limit of epoxied stained glass "stones" applied one by one to the glass. Their colors repeat colors of the paint.

When the epoxy on the glass bits has dried completely, the glass panel is *turned over.* The back of the glass is painted freely and quickly with transparent glass stain in marine colors over the entire area except the space occupied by the fish. It is left free of background paint to assure brightness of colors on the fish.

Reverse Painting Under Glass

Underglass painting of mirrors and clock faces as well as framed glass paintings backed with delicately colored velvet was popular from the eighteenth through the nineteenth century in New England, Pennsylvania, and a few midwestern states. Typical early American homes were not plain, severe, and colorless, as they have sometimes been represented. In reality, from earliest times the homes and furnishings of our ancestors were ablaze with vivid color, imagination, gay design, and lively humor. Red, russet, yellow, blue, and gray exteriors; floors and woodwork of pumpkin, red, blue, and green with stenciled patterns; walls of rose, gray, and yellow with stenciled designs or bright painted landscapes; gay printed fabrics and patterned carpets enlivened the early homes of colonial times. Accessories too, such as painted and stenciled picture frames, clocks, and mirrors accented the decorating schemes. The decorative and charming reverse-painted mirror in simple homespun folk style is delightfully and equally appropriate in suburban or country homes of today.

Many of the mirrors and clock faces originally were sold to householders by itinerant salesmen. But talented homemakers with little or no art training found these flat glass paintings easy to copy and decorate with bright-colored oil paints. Although the paintings are not difficult for the novice, time and meticulous care are required to apply the effective delicate lines and flowing brushstrokes. Because the painted design is applied to the underside of the glass and must be done in reverse order, highlights and shadows are painted on the glass first instead of being applied as finishing strokes. When these details are painted and dry, main colors are applied and the backgrounds are added. Traditionally, the last step was to back the completed painting with a thin coat of off-white paint.

MAKING A MIRROR FRAME

The first step in making an underglass painting for a mirror is to *select or make the frame.* A sheet of double-strength window glass is cut to fit exactly the top quarter of the area within the mirror frame. The remainder of the area will be filled by the mirror. If too much of the framed area is taken up by the underglass painting, part of your face reflection may be cut off at the top. The mirror frame illustrated for the demonstration project begins as a plain flat rabbeted frame. Half-round turned posts, made by separating an unfinished table leg down the center with a saw, are glued to the front of each side of the frame. Small wood blocks and narrow shelflike strips are glued top and bottom. The frame is painted leaf green.

PREPARING THE REVERSE DESIGN

When you have cut and cleaned the glass, it is time to *prepare your reversed design* pattern. Draw in outline form the design you will paint, filling in the space well. If you like, you may leave space for a painted decorative border around the picture. There is considerable latitude suitable for modern adaptations of underglass reverse painting. All sorts of designs were used traditionally in these pictures, such as famous or fashionable homes, farms, winter or summer landscapes or seascapes, and portraits. Flower arrangements were especially popular. Whatever inter-

ests you most is a design possibility. Boats, antique cars or fire engines, sport scenes, humorous situations, famous buildings, and portraits of famous persons are all good subjects for reverse paintings under glass.

Make an exact copy of the completed drawing on tracing paper, then go over its lines with a fine-pointed black felt-tipped marker. A painting in full color is helpful, too. Position it nearby so you may refer to it as you paint the color areas in reverse on the glass. The next step is to turn the tracing paper outline over to its opposite side on the white table surface or over a light box, if you have one. Position the clean glass on top of the reversed tracing paper and tape them togehter at several points. Or you may prefer to trace the design in reverse onto drawing paper and secure the glass to it for a guide. Either way, emphasize the lines with a marker.

THE REVERSE PAINTING

Before you begin to paint, place your working light so no reflection is cast on the glass. Mix a small amount of black tube paint with some spar varnish and a drop or two of turpentine. With a #0 liner brush, trace all the black outlines onto the glass with thin delicate strokes. Leave them undisturbed until the paint has dried for about 24 hours.

The next step is to paint all the highlights and shadows in your picture first. Where colors of ensuing layers of paint will overlap, there must be at least a day or longer of drying time between layers. By the time you paint the final background colors of the the picture, you will have covered most of the design on the back of the glass. For a neat finish, apply a thin coat of off-white paint overall.

In the demonstrated project, colors were applied as follows: (1) highlights on the water, brown shadows on the boat sails, brown cabin and small figures on the boat; (2) red paint on the boat, flag, and small buildings on the far shore; (3) green trees and light ocher on sails and building roof; (4) light green on fields, nearest hills, and part of the water; (5) dark blue water and distant dark green hills; (6) sky colors and light blue water. The paints were allowed to dry between each group of colors applied. The colors are mostly flat in the manner of early folk paintings found on well-preserved old mirrors.

Thin lines are traced on the glass above the drawing with a #0 liner brush and oil paint mixture. Protect the glass from finger marks.

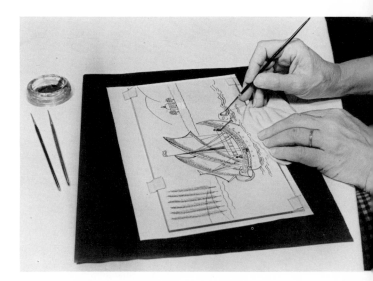

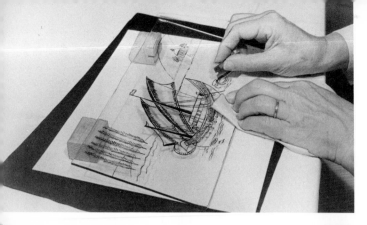

When the paint is dry, refine the lines with a single-edged razor blade. The glass is elevated with small blocks so the lines are seen clearly. If you have access to a light table, shadows cast by the painted lines are eliminated and no props are necessary.

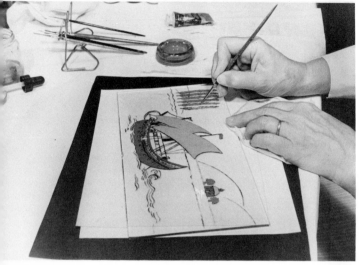

Colors are painted in the reverse order of sequence that is customary for conventional painting, because this underglass painting will be turned over when it is installed in its frame. Green is painted on top of details of tree forms. Boat sails are painted on top of their shadows.

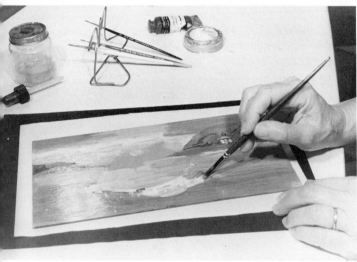

By the time final background colors are applied, most of the design has been covered up back of the painting.

The completed underglass painting.

When the reverse glass painting is completed, it is time to install it and the mirror within the prepared frame. A thin strip of wood, 1/4" thick by 1/2" wide by 12" long (equal to the width of the frame opening plus the rabbet recesses) is sanded with very fine sandpaper. It is wiped clean of sanding dust, then shellacked. When the shellac has dried, it is gilded with rub-on paste gold or other gold paint. The wood strip is installed between the underglass painting at the top of the frame and the mirror below it. To install the wood strip, the painting, and the mirror, the frame is laid flat on a tabletop, face down. Carefully position the glass painting face down in the frame opening, fitting it snugly against the top of the frame with its edges resting on the rabbeting, top and sides. Mark the exact location where the *lower edge* of the painted glass extends over the rabbet on each side of the frame. Remove the glass, then glue or tack the wood strip into place with its top edge resting exactly on the marks you just made on the rabbeting. The remaining area of the frame opening below the wood crosspiece is measured meticulously so the mirror will fit the space. A section of mirror, cut to fit, is installed below the crosspiece. Then the painted glass is lowered gently into the space above the crosspiece. To hold the glass secure, little triangular metal *glazier's points* (available in hardware stores) are pressed into the frame all around the glass, flat against it. The glass is backed with firm cardboard or plywood tacked into the frame. If desired, additional gilt can be applied to the front of the frame.

Carefully position the completed and dried painting face down in the top back of the frame opening.

Install a wood strip with ends resting on the recessed rabbet and fitting snugly up against the bottom edge of the painting. Glue or tack it into place.

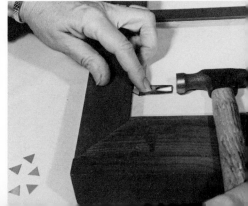

Heavy wide masking tape is applied to the back of the glass around its edge to protect it when "glazier's points" are tapped into the frame flat against the glass. A special little gadget is placed against a flat edge of a glazier point and it is tapped in with a hammer. The metal gadget is flat at one end, humped at the opposite end. See illustration.

Finished reverse painting in mirror frame.

The clockface and small panel below it are reverse-painted and gilded by Wilma Cymbala.

Unusual clock with three gilded and reverse-painted panels. Wilma Cymbala. Owned by Mrs. Richard Minnich.

Framed panel. Reverse-painted and gilded. Wilma Cymbala.

Painting Three-Dimensional Glass, Unfired

A special problem is encountered when you paint three-dimensional glassware. Obviously, the guiding sketch must be anchored back of the curved glass surface in such a way that the lines to be followed with the paintbrush are not distorted. Make vertical cuts along the bottom and/or top of the pattern guide when necessary so the paper can be fitted into the curvature of the glass (see illustration). Press the pattern against the inside surface of the glass, allowing the cuts to overlap where the glass narrows. Hold the pattern steady, then tape it to the inside of the glass with masking tape.

A handy little pad can be slipped inside the tumbler and held firmly against the back of the paper pattern with two or three fingers pressing the pattern in place against the glass. It eliminates distortion of the guiding lines while you paint the glass. The pad is made from a child's sock with the top cut away at the ankle. Stuff the foot section with cotton and sew it shut at the cut end or bind it with a rubber band. With the pad in position, paint above the outlines with a #1 soft pointed brush and the oil paint mixture. When the lines have set, the colors are filled in: light and dark green on two leaves and the stem in the demonstration lily-of-the-valley project with white blooms on the lily. When the paint dries, second coats are applied and dried. An extra stem and an outlined leaf are gilded with Liquid Leaf.

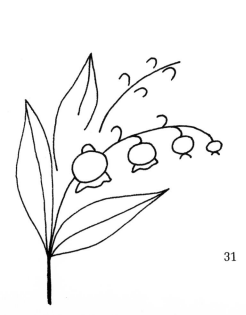

31

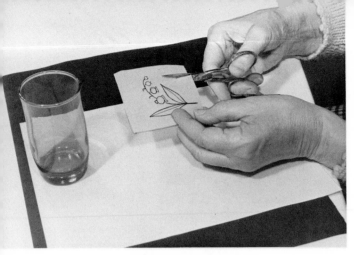

Make vertical cuts along the lower edge of the paper pattern guide so it can be fitted into the curvature of the glass.

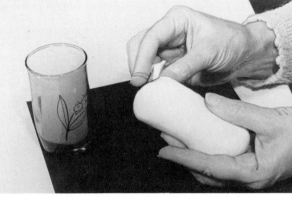

Make a small pad to fit against the back of the pattern.

Tape the pattern to the inside of the glass with masking tape.

Hold the pad in position while you trace on the glass over the outlines with a #1 tracing brush and oil paint mixture. The small finger braces against the glass.

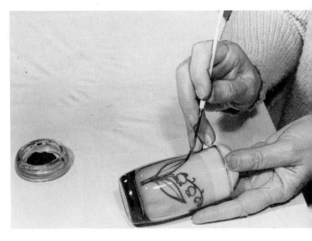

The tall glass is painted with deep rose-colored blossoms, green leaves, brown stems, and gilded highlights on a turquoise glass. The short glass has shaded white lily-of-the-valley blossoms, green and chartreuse leaves and unfired gold highlights, on tinted glass.

Bright blue glass cannister with sparkling painted design. Wilma Cymbala.

A city scene is painted in the round so designs on all sides of the glass complement one another. Wilma Cymbala.

Fired Glass Decoration

Many of the projects in this book do not require a kiln. The range of glass decorating techniques is extended considerably, however, if you have access to a kiln. Although unfired glass painting is lovely and durable, the most permanent effects are achieved with fired glass paints or

PILGRIM BOTTLE. Venice, Italy (sixteenth century.) Gilded and enameled in gold, blue, red, and white. Height 13⅝". *Photograph by courtesy of The Toledo Museum of Art. Gift of Edward Drummond Libbey.*

enamels. It is important to note here that dissimilar kinds and colors of glass will not remain fused together for such methods as embossing or lamination. They can be fired separately to round their edges, then they can be bonded together with special epoxy made for bonding glass to glass.* The ensuing discussion of firing decorated glass is general. Specific directions are detailed in related sections.

Ceramic, metal-enameling, or glass kilns that have pyrometers and temperature controls are suitable for firing glass. Although some crafts-men employ pyrometric clay cones for testing temperatures in firing simple glass projects, for best results the kiln is equipped with a pyrome-ter. Kiln switches are operated several times during some of the more complex processes. The use of several cones to indicate different heating adjustments can be awkward; it permits only partial temperature control.

Flat molds on which decorated glassware will be placed for firing are sliced from soft *insulation brick* (not firebrick) with a fine-toothed hack-saw. The top surface of each brick mold is rubbed with kiln wash to fill the pores of the brick and make a smooth surface. It can be further leveled smooth with a long flat spatula. Kiln wash provides an important separa-tor between the glass and brick mold which prevents the glass from sticking to the brick when the kiln is fired. Although sheet glass can be fired directly on a kiln shelf that has been treated with kiln wash, three-dimensional glassware should be supported on a section of the insulation brick to assure that it heats as evenly as possible.

Like ceramic ware, glass is placed in a cold kiln for any kind of firing. All glass requires that the kiln be vented until the temperature reaches approximately 950°F. This means leaving a peephole open and the door slightly ajar. Atmospheric moisture in the kiln and in the room, as well as gases from the chemicals in the decorating materials, can cloud the heating glassware if they cannot escape quickly. By venting the kiln while it begins heating, you assure that all these fumes escape as speedily as possible. In addition, venting the kiln at this time prevents the tempera-ture from rising too rapidly at first and perhaps breaking the glass. This precaution is especially vital for stemmed ware and other pieces with narrow projections. The narrower portions heat more rapidly than broad or thick parts of a glass object and may crack if the kiln is fired too fast.

When the glassware has been decorated and dried, it is ready for firing. Set it on one of the prepared flat molds or directly on the kiln shelf which has been treated with kiln wash. Position the glass in a cold kiln away from the door, if the kiln is a front loader, so parts of the glass nearest the kiln door do not remain cooler than the rest of the piece.

Turn the kiln switch to "LOW" and vent the door for a gentle preheat-ing period as described, by leaving the door ajar and a peephole open. After two hours, or at 450°F, turn the switch or switches to "HIGH" and close the peephole, but leave the door *ajar.* The "MEDIUM" switch is seldom used in firing glass. In many kilns, it turns off half the elements, making for very uneven heating; it sets up considerable strain in glass that makes it brittle and easily broken. At 950°F, *close the door* tightly for the re-mainder of the firing period. If the decorated glassware is being fired to 1100°, the kiln is shut off as soon as it reaches that temperature. If the temperature tends to rise a little from heat that is stored in the walls of

The top of each flat insulation brick mold is sifted or rubbed with kiln wash for a separator to prevent glass from sticking. It can be smoothed with a long flat spatula.

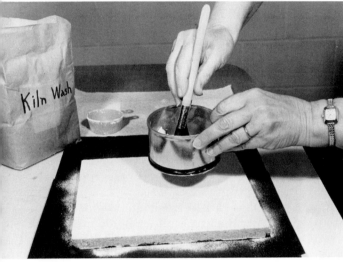

Glass can be fired directly on a kiln shelf that is sifted or painted with kiln wash.

the kiln, open the door a crack to hold it down. Then close the door tightly. It must be remembered that three-dimensional ware that has been pre-formed will probably distort as it heats above 1150° or 1200°F. This discussion concerns glass articles that are being decorated, not bent. Flat glass can be taken to a higher temperature when it is being fired flat for decoration, even though it is not being bent, because it rests flat on the shelf or mold and cannot distort.

When the temperature drops to 1000°F, turn the switch on "LOW" to hold the temperature within the "annealing range" for a half hour to an hour. This relieves strain in the glass which results from being fired. The temperature will drop very slowly as it descends between 1000° and 900°F. Although the annealing range temperature differs slightly among glass types, nearly all will anneal somewhere between these two temperatures. Glass that is not annealed when it is fired may tend to be brittle and easily broken. Very small glass pieces such as the "jewels" fired from scraps of stained glass will usually anneal automatically as the kiln cools.

After the glass has annealed, the kiln is turned off and is left to cool naturally. If the kiln temperature tends to drop rapidly, it is advisable to turn it back on "LOW" for about five minutes from time to time to slow it down to about a 20° drop every five to seven minutes, as a safety precaution against breakage. Do not open the kiln door until it is cool.

The firing directions discussed here apply to small or medium-sized glass articles and medium-sized firing loads. Commercial production of many large wares or heavy loads in a large kiln are not within the scope of this book.

METALLIC PAINTS, FIRED

Fired metallic lusters applied to glass projects in this book are Liquid Bright Gold and Liquid Palladium (for a silver finish), the kinds for decorating vitreous enamels and glass. They can be bought in most ceramic supply stores, In general, they reach maturity at about 1100°F. Most glass will not soften at that temperature. If you plan to gild a set of several glasses, test-fire one of them to learn how it reacts to 1100°F temperature before proceeding. If it is fired too hot, it may collapse.

Luster essence, made for thinning these metallic paints, for cleaning the small brushes and ruling pens, or for removing gilt errors from work, should be obtained when the metallic luster is bought. *Follow the same routine* for these fired metallics that is recommended for applying unfired gilt: small sable brushes, anchoring the bottles to keep them from falling over, cleaning the glass, and working over a sketch taped under the glass. The bottles of luster and essence must be kept covered; they are very volatile and will evaporate rapidly. Dip the brush into the gold paint and touch it lightly to the inside of the bottle neck to remove excess paint. Brush it quickly on the glass, following the sketch lines underneath it. If you should make an error, it is advisable to remove all the gilt with Luster Essence and begin again. Wipe it off two or three times to make sure the glass is clean. Avoid retracing a stroke to emphasize it. If you want a second coat, fire the first coat, then apply another.

When the luster has been applied, set the glass in a warm place to dry for an hour or longer. While it is drying, read again the foregoing section "Fired Glass Decoration" for instructions about preparation of a firing base and how to fire the kiln. When the kiln begins to heat you may notice some luster fumes emanating from it as they are driven off by the rise in temperature. The fumes are not harmful and they will soon disperse.

Fired metallic lusters can be fired several times without harming their beauty, just as long as they are not overfired at too high a temperature.

To gild a band around a lid or container, anchor it to a banding wheel with small wads of modeling clay as shown here. Revolve the wheel with one hand while the other hand is braced and holds the brush motionless.

The wide beveled edge of this old-fashioned ice-cream boat is gilded with two coats of liquid gold with firing between coats.

Blown glass open form is gilded with fired palladium design. Blown glass and gilt by Polly Rothenberg.

SGRAFFITO DESIGNS, FIRED

Sgraffito is a linear decoration produced by scratching a design through a surface layer of unfired glaze, enamel, or paint to reveal a different colored ground beneath it. When the scratched design is completed, the piece is fired in a kiln. Sgraffito commonly appears on pottery and metal enamels; it has interesting potential as a glass decoration. It can be done in either brushed glass paint or sifted glass enamels.

In the demonstration project, a two-dimensional free-form shape in yellow stained glass is taped over a broadly outlined pattern base. Black glass decorating color blended with squeegee oil is traced on the glass over the outlines with a #1 pointed brush. As soon as the paint has set, black fill-in color is applied within the outlines to paint broad areas that will be sgraffitoed in a pattern. The color is painted with a #3 liner brush. It is dried in an oven at 200°F for about fifteen minutes or until it is dry. It cannot be sgraffitoed while it is damp. For this technique, use a sharp pointed pencil or other scribing point to draw a freehand, mostly linear design through the dry paint to expose the stained glass color. Gently whisk away dry crumbs of paint with a soft brush. Fire the glass to 1100°F. When it has cooled, it is epoxied to a clear glass base prepared previously with a loop hanger fired to it under a small tab of glass.

To make this clear glass base, cut a piece of window glass in the same shape, but slightly larger than the stained glass, with a 3/4" clearance all around it. With dabs of Elmer's Glue-All, cement a small tab of the same glass to the top edge of the clear glass panel over a nichrome wire loop for a hanger. The glue will hold them in position while they are transported to the kiln. Fire the clear glass to 1350°F, and let it cool in the kiln.

Stained glass cannot be fused to clear glass because of the difference in their coefficients (rates) of expansion. To do so would result in the two kinds of glass cracking apart some time after they cool. But they are frequently fired separately, then bonded with epoxy to make complex panels or medallions.

Broad areas are painted black and dried in an oven for about fifteen minutes.

A pattern is sketched to guide the scratched sgraffito design. The scribing is done freehand.

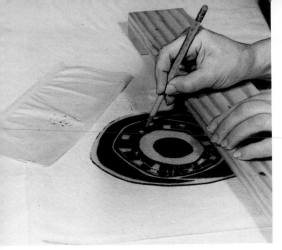

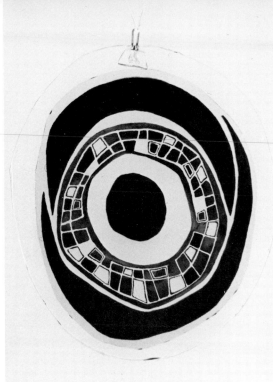

A sharp pointed pencil cuts through the dry paint. Keep the point clean by wiping it on a paper tissue near at hand.

The sgraffitoed yellow stained glass free-form medallion is fired, then it is epoxied to clear glass. Fired glass and wire hanger.

ENAMELING THREE-DIMENSIONAL GLASS

Fine glass enamel and gilt wares were among the more elegant fired glass styles developed by early Romans and later revived by the Venetians. Over the years, glassworkers of many nations copied them with variations in their own indigenous styles. In the recent past, the influence of formal Swedish crystal glass was responsible for an innovation in world glass fashions; sparse decoration tended to complement the beauty

Glass goblet. Newcastle-on-Tyne, England. William Beilby and Ralph Beilby (c. 1765.) Clear glass enameled in colors. 7" tall. *Photograph by courtesy of The Toledo Museum of Art. Gift of Edward Drummond Libbey.*

and brilliance of the transparent glass itself. Today a revival of interest in ornamentation has encouraged a desire for color and pattern in glass of all kinds. The American Bicentennial Celebration has brought forth formal and folk styles of our colonial heritage, as well as designs inspired by works of our Old World ancestors. But not much has been written about actual techniques of decorating this glassware. Even the novice can decorate lovely glass forms with reliable and durable fired paints, developed in beautiful colors by modern chemistry.

The first three-dimensional enamel project begins with one of a group of empty, transparent, dark blue glass cosmetic containers, to be painted in brushed white enamel and gold luster. The vessels are washed thoroughly inside and outside to remove remnants of cosmetics and paper labels. Then they are placed in a kiln on sections of insulation brick that has been rubbed or sifted with kiln wash (see "Fired Glass Decoration") and fired to 1100°F to burn out any remaining chemicals and to assure that the glass can be fired to 1100° without collapsing. It would be a shame to paint beautiful designs on the glass, only to see it collapse in the kiln. When the switch is turned off, the glass is left to cool in the kiln overnight.

To enamel a form like the blue flask container, draw a suitable outline design that fills the space nicely. Because the glass color is dark, white transfer paper can be used to trace the design onto the bottle. White graphite paper, sold by the sheet or by the roll, is usually available at art supply stores. The white transfer paper used for the illustrated project is Singer Dressmaker's Tracing Paper, bought at a sewing center. It works very well. Cut the design paper and the white transfer paper to fit the space and tape them securely to the glass surface.

For the demonstrated project, a hard sharp pencil point is traced firmly over the outlines of the small floral shapes and the ribs of the small leaf sprays to transfer them to the bottle surface. The tiny leaves will be applied freehand in one stroke each with a #0 fine red sable brush. The

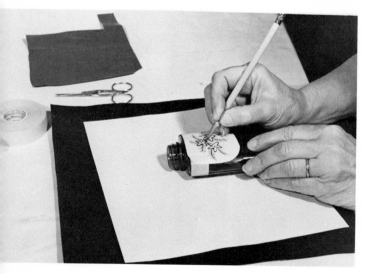

A sharp hard pencil point is traced firmly over the outlines of the small floral shapes and ribs of the diminutive leaf sprays.

glass enamels applied on these fired projects are powdered glass decorating colors (see "Supply Sources") in the LOW FIRE series that fire to 1100°. They are made especially for preformed glassware and flat glass that withstand that temperature without being deformed. The powdered paints have many minute lumps that must be pressed out with an artist's tiny paint spatula. A very small amount of the powder, lifted out of the container on the end of the same oil paint spatula, is mixed with two or three drops of squeegee oil. It is blended thoroughly for several minutes to eliminate unevenness and tiny lumps. Although water or enameling gum can be mixed with the powder in place of the oil, they tend to dry rapidly and must be applied quickly to achieve a smooth application. The next step is to roll a #1 or #0 sable tracer, liner, or other fine brush in the prepared enamel and outline the design over the traced white lines on the blue glass flask. White enamel is employed for this initial project. When squeegee oil is the medium, the enameled design should be dried in a 200°F oven.

At least two or three coats of enamel, with firings in between, are required to achieve the remarkably rich effect attained by early Venetian glassworkers. They worked with handmade tools and enamels they ground themselves. Today, by working with a heat-controlled kiln and the fine powdered enamels developed in beautiful uniform colors by modern chemistry, you will be delighted with the lovely enamel-decorated glass you can achieve, if you follow a few precise instructions.

After you have applied your first enamel coat within the outlines you applied with your brush (in the same color), set it in a 200°F oven for five to ten minutes or longer if needed until the paint is dry. Then inspect it closely. If there are areas where you want to carve away some of the dry paint, a very sharp, hard pencil point will do the job. Do not go over the unfired paint with a touch-up brush. It will not be smooth and it will show up in the firing. After the first firing, when the glass has cooled, a second smooth coat is applied over the first coat. The paint fires translucent, even after two or three additional coats. Thin areas can be meticulously covered in the second coat and fired; then a third coat is fired over all. Fire to 1100°F, carefully following directions that deal with kiln-fired glass decoration detailed earlier. Let the kiln cool completely before the glass is removed.

A fine brush outlines the designs in white glass-decorating color blended with squeegee oil. It is baked in a 150°F oven to dry, before it is fired to 1100°.

After the first fill-in coat is fired, a second smooth coat of white is applied and fired. Notice how the bottle is anchored by the third finger inside the bottle and the little finger on the right hand bracing.

When three coats have been fired on the blue bottle, small gold dots in the flower centers and a few strokes on the leaf stems of the design are added with gold luster and fired again to 1100°. The metal bottle cap on the container is gilded with two coats of Liquid Leaf or other *unfired* gilt. There should be four hours drying time between these two coats of gold.

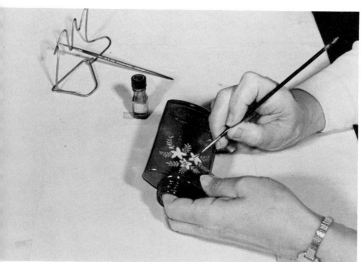

After three coats of white paint are applied and fired on the flowers (2 coats on leaves), small gold dots in the flower centers and thin gold strokes on leaf stems are added with luster and fired to 1100°F.

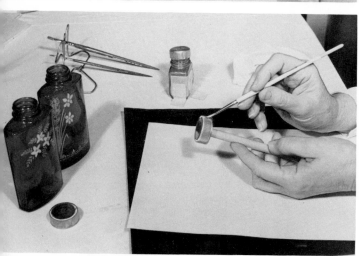

The plastic bottle caps are gilded with two coats of Liquid Leaf gilt. There must be four hours' drying time between coats to prevent the second coat from loosening the first.

A handsome pair of dark blue transparent glass bottles are enameled in white and gold (fired.) Caps are gilded.

Individual patterns are taped behind the glass on three-dimensional glassware where designs are repetitive. These unit patterns are much easier to manipulate than a large pattern. The illustrated *Bicentennial glass mug* is enameled with a broad red stripe down the outside of the handle, a wide blue band around the base, and large white stars on the side. The stars are positioned so the ones seen through the glass fit the overall scheme. An individual paper pattern is taped behind the glass for each star in turn. Although the little pad can be applied against this small pattern, it is not essential. With a #0 pointed brush, two thin lines of liquid gold are applied top and bottom in existing indentations in the glass. The mug is fired to 1100°F after each color application. All colors have two coats. Glass objects like this, which have applied parts (the handles), should be fired very slowly so they do not crack apart either when firing or when cooling.

Individual small pattern guides are easy to anchor inside the mug.

A wide red stripe is enameled down the outside edge of the glass handle.

Bicentennial mug. Red stripe
down the handle, white stars,
blue band around the base. Thin
lines of liquid gold are applied top
and bottom in existing indentations. The mug is fired to 1100°F
after *each* color application. All
colors have two fired coats.

Enameled amber goblet. All colors fired. Polly Rothenberg.

3

* Embossing
Glass

Stained Glass Bonded to Clear Glass

Stained-glass shapes are embossed in relief on clear sheet glass or three-dimensional glass objects by adhering them with a clear epoxy cement made especially for bonding glass to glass. Double-strength plate and window glasses are suitable as the base for embossed sheet projects. Almost any three-dimensional clear glass articles with plain level surface areas can be embossed with stained glass shapes. The undulating surface of antique stained glass, which gives it character and beauty, can sometimes leave irregular bubbles in the epoxy between the clear glass base and shallow depressions in the stained glass. Although they can be quite decorative, if you do not care for this effect, rolled cathedral glass has one smooth surface, suitable for bubble-free bonding.

For an initial project on flat glass or a three-dimensional object that has flat surfaces, draw a design that is composed of very simple shapes and that nicely fills the space to be embossed. Trace the outlines of the shapes onto firm paper such as stiff drawing paper and cut them out, carefully following the lines. They are the templates that will guide you in cutting out small stained-glass pieces. (Read again the section "Cutting Glass.") When all the glass is cut, the sharp edges should be blunted. They may either be sanded very lightly with extrafine *wettable* carborundum paper under water, or fired in a ceramic or enameling kiln to smooth the sharp edges.

Prefiring Stained Glass for Embossing

Flat molds on which the glass is fired are sliced from soft *insulation brick* with a fine-toothed hacksaw. The top surface of the mold is rubbed gently with powdered kiln wash which fills the pores in the brick to make a smooth surface. Sift additional kiln wash over it, then level it off with a long flat spatula to make the firing surface as smooth as possible. Between firings, smooth it again with the flat spatula. After several firings, scrape it off and apply fresh kiln wash, available in ceramic supply shops. Kiln wash serves as a good separator between the glass and the mold to prevent the glass from sticking to the brick when the kiln is fired. The next step is to position the glass pieces.

Pick up each clean stained-glass shape with small tweezers and gently lower them onto the prepared brick mold surface, without disturbing the separator powder. The mold with its load of glass is positioned on a nichrome wire mesh firing rack and is transported to the kiln with a firing fork. The kiln has *not yet been turned on.* Set the rack in the center of the kiln shelf with the smallest glass pieces toward the front loading door so they do not overfire. Leave the door ajar for ventilation and turn the controls to "LOW" until the temperature reaches 450°F, then turn to "HIGH." At 950°, *close the door.* Stained-glass edges should be blunted by 1300°. Turn off the kiln and ventilate the door for a few moments to halt the rise in temperature. Finally, close the door tightly. Let the kiln cool naturally to room temperature.

Epoxying the Glass

Remove the glass from the kiln, wash it in warm water to remove any clinging kiln wash, and dry it thoroughly. The next step is to cement the stained glass to its clean glass base. Both fired stained glass and unfired pieces with edges blunted by sanding are bonded for embossed designs in the same way. The workroom temperature and all materials involved in epoxying should be maintained between 75° and 80°F throughout the entire process. A cooler temperature will slow the setting considerably. Ventilate the work area so epoxy fumes are not inhaled excessively.

Work must be done on a level table and remain undisturbed for 24 hours after completion. If the table is not level, pieces of epoxied glass are sure to slide slowly out of position while they are drying. Check them occasionally; if any have moved, slide them gently back into position as long as they move easily.

Epoxy cement comes in two containers; one holds the resin and the other the hardener. Mix only the amount for the project in hand. Its adhesive property will begin to activate as soon as it is mixed. The epoxy may start to set as soon as 20 to 30 minutes thereafter. It may be bought in tubes for small projects.* Epoxy solvent should be bought at the same

*Thermoset Resin #600 and Hardener #37 are used for projects in this book.

time. Follow directions on the container. Some brands may require different blending.

Before you begin epoxying, clear the worktable. Assemble the adhesive, the glass base to be embossed, stained-glass shapes, a small container similar in size to a baby food jar *lid* for blending the epoxy, some round toothpicks or other spreading sticks, and a roll of paper towels. An unopened can of epoxy solvent should be available; it must be kept closed when it is not in use because it is volatile.

Tape the design pattern underneath the glass to guide your placement of each colored glass segment. When it is secured in exactly the position you want it, it is time to blend the epoxy resin and hardener in very small amounts so the adhesive is used up before it sets. For small projects, the equivalent of 1/8 teaspoon each makes a considerable amount. If you find that you have not mixed enough, it is simple to blend additional adhesive. Beginners tend to mix too much at first. Any remainder must be discarded. (Do not contaminate unmixed resin with any of the hardener in the original containers.)

As soon as the epoxy is blended, spread a thin coat of it evenly on the underside of a cleaned stained glass piece, position it on the clear glass base, and press it firmly into place. Continue the process of spreading epoxy, positioning glass, and pressing firmly. If some of the adhesive seeps between the glass, it will harden into transparency and not be noticed. When all the glass is applied, check it from time to time to see whether any pieces have moved. This precaution is especially important for three-dimensional objects whose flat surfaces may not be absolutely even. Glass that may have shifted is slid back into position as long as the adhesive has not set and offers little resistance when you move the glass. Leave the paper pattern guide under the embossed glass until it is firmly attached to the clear glass base. Then if any move, it will be easy to slide them back into position over the pattern. Clean off the tops of glass shapes and around the outside of the embossed area on the glass base when the epoxy has set, but before it hardens. It is scraped away with a single-edge razor blade, then wiped clean with a paper towel dampened with a little solvent; the solvent must not run under or between the applied glass segments. Embossing glass is easy if directions are carefully followed. The ensuing demonstrated projects suggest several techniques for this simple but enchanting process.

DESERT ROADRUNNER

Desert Roadrunner is a basic example of stained-glass fragments epoxied to colorless double-strength window glass, premeasured to fit a small window. A full-size drawing is traced onto stiff paper to make templates for cutting glass shapes as described earlier. Edges of the smallest glass segments are sanded under water to remove thin slivers that may be hazardous to the fingers. In order to retain the crisp effect desired for this special design, edges are not blunted by kiln firing. The glass base is washed in detergent water, rinsed, and dried. To facilitate drying the smallest stained-glass segments, they are washed and spread on a sheet of kitchen foil and dried in an oven at 200°. Glass must be thoroughly dry before it is epoxied.

The clean window glass base is taped over a full-size outline sketch of the roadrunner. A very thin coat of epoxy is spread over the underside of glass shapes for body, head, and beak. They are positioned on the glass base over the sketch. Each stained-glass piece is pressed into place. The cluster of small crest segments that give the bird its sprightly appearance are dabbed with bits of epoxy and also pressed into place. It is not necessary to completely cover the underside of these small pieces with the cement. To do so makes them awkward to handle without smearing adhesive over fingers and glass and causing a difficult clean-up job. Each piece is given a few dabs of epoxy with a toothpick, positioned with tweezers, and pressed into position. When the adhesive sets, additional glass chips are cemented over the head and body to give a fuller three-dimensional effect. The bird's eye is made with unfired paint. When the window panel is completed, it is left to dry for several hours on a *level* table where the room temperature is around 75°F. Fused glass and wire hangers can be epoxied to the top corners of the panel if desired.

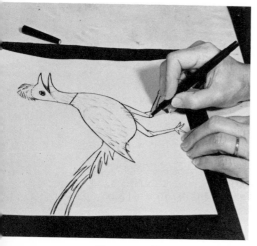

A full-sized drawing is traced onto stiff paper to make templates for cutting out stained glass shapes.

The clean window glass base is taped over a full-sized outline sketch of the roadrunner. Epoxy is spread *thinly* over the underside of each piece in turn and it is pressed firmly into place over the outlines beneath the glass base.

Very small stained glass segments are picked up with broad-tipped tweezers to avoid getting epoxy over hands and fingers.

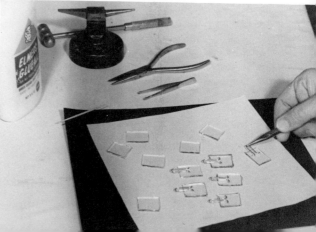

To make a fused glass and wire hanger, the first step is to glue a tiny silver wire loop (20-gauge) to a small tab of glass so the loop end extends beyond the glass.

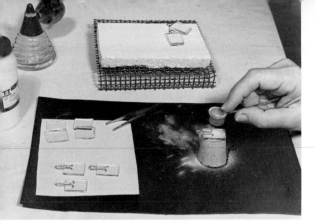 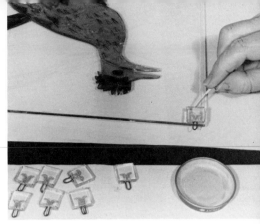

Sift clear glass enamel (flux) on the wire and glass. It will speed the fusing process. Set a second glass piece on top, and fire on a section of insulation brick or directly on the kiln shelf that has been coated with kiln wash. Fire to 1450°–1500°F to fuse the glass and wire together.

A fused glass and wire hanger is epoxied and positioned on each top corner of the glass. Let it dry overnight.

DESERT ROADRUNNER, CLOWN OF THE WEST.

THE BOTTLES PANEL

The *Bottles* panel combines embossed stained-glass segments bonded within unfired overlapping painted bottles. Two copies of a drawing are made. A clean sheet of double-strength window glass is taped over one drawing. On the second copy, outlines of the planned stained-glass shapes are drawn within each bottle; the outlines are traced onto firm paper and cut into templates. When each piece of stained glass has been cut out around a template and the edges are sanded under water to smooth them, they are washed, rinsed, and dried. To prepare paint for brushing the bottle outlines on the glass base, blend equal parts of artist's tube oil paint (about 1/8") and spar varnish with two or three drops of turpentine, as described under "Unfired Paints." With a #3 liner brush, paint the bottle outlines carefully on the clear glass over the drawing taped under the glass. When the paint is dry, scrape away irregularities in the paint with a single-edged razor blade or sharp stencil knife. The next step is to prepare epoxy adhesive that will cement the stained glass in place.

Blend about 1/4 teaspoon each of epoxy resin and hardener, following the manufacturer's instructions on the containers. The underside of each piece of glass is given a thin coat of adhesive and is pressed firmly into place on the clear glass base. When the epoxy has set but is not hard, excess cement is scraped away with a razor blade and wiped clean with a *small amount* of epoxy solvent on a cloth.

Two copies of the above drawing are made, one on stiff paper.

The stiff paper drawing is cut into templates around which stained glass shapes are cut.

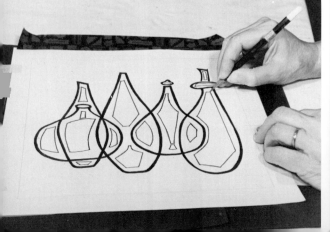

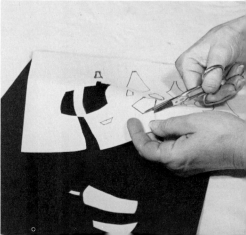

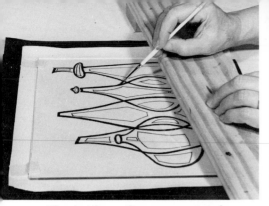 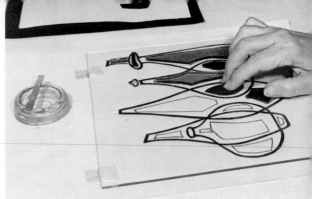

The bottle outlines are painted carefully on clear window glass with a #3 liner.

Each stained glass is epoxied and pressed firmly in place.

Front panel for an epoxied glass box.

THREE-DIMENSIONAL COVERED GLASS CANISTER

The *three-dimensional covered glass canister* has plain flat surfaces, suitable for stained-glass embossing. The simple geometric plan for each side is composed of small squares and triangles cut from stained-glass scraps. There will be no grout between glass segments because the planned effect is a raised design rather than a mosaic. The result is lighter and more sparkling; grout tends to keep some of the light rays from penetrating the colored glass. A few deep or bright glass colors assure that the result is not too pastel.

A pattern guide is drawn full scale and traced onto stiff paper from which glass-cutting templates are made. The pattern itself is taped inside the canister under each side surface *in turn* as it is embossed and dried. The next step is to prepare the small colored glass triangles and squares; several extra pieces are cut and the best ones selected. The softly blunted corners of kiln-fired glass seem most suitable for the canister's rounded corners, so all the glass is fired according to directions given at the beginning of this embossing section. Because the stained glass is set closely together in the design, the surface design area of each canister side is spread with cement instead of the underside of each glass piece. Glass is picked up with tweezers, positioned, and pressed into place, until all are applied. Each surface of the canister is dried completely before the next side is embossed.

Small triangles and squares are cut from stained glass.

The glass segments are placed on a section of insulation brick that was sifted with kiln wash for a separator.

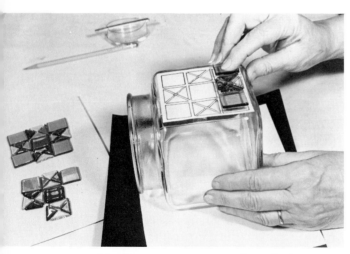

The design pattern is taped inside the cannister. The fired glass squares and triangles are epoxied to the glass.

The pattern is moved to each side in turn until the last side of the cannister is decorated.

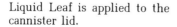

Liquid Leaf is applied to the cannister lid.

A rounded jar is laid horizontal and anchored between two sticks tacked to a board. Stained glass is epoxied along the top horizontal plane. The adhesive for each row of glass must set before the next row is applied on a horizontal plane to make sure that the glass bits do not slide down the jar.

The completed project.

The completed jar with grouting that was pressed in between glass pieces with a rubber spatula. Extra-small glass is applied on top of some of the stained glass shapes to give a sculptured effect.

COTTAGE RETREAT PICTURE

For the *Cottage Retreat* project, small stained-glass shapes, prefired to blunt their edges, make colorful jewellike segments for composing a stained-glass picture on a double-strength window glass background. Scraps of stained glass left from other projects should be saved. Even the tiniest bits that are fired to 1350°F, as described earlier, become glistening gems that are useful as epoxied and embossed petals, leaves, and buds for diminutive flowers, or for sparkling accents in an otherwise bland design.

Whenever a project is fired, some of these glass bits can be fired along with other pieces, then stored for future use.

The window glass base for this picture project is colored with transparent glass enamels that are fired in a kiln. When the panel has been washed and dried, a stencil cut from a commercial paper towel (not the soft stretchy kind) is wet and laid over the lower part as illustrated in the photograph. The exposed sky area is sprayed with enameling gum or liquid agar, diluted three parts water to one part gum or agar. This solution should go through an aerosol sprayer without clogging or sputtering. Be sure the sprayer is kept clean. Hold the glass at arm's length and spray in light puffs so the liquid does not puddle or run. As soon as the glass is sprayed, granular 80-mesh low-fire transparent turquoise *glass* enamel is sifted in three thin applications, with light spraying between the layers. The stencil is removed with tweezers. The glass is dried and fired to 1250°F on a kiln shelf that has been sifted with kiln wash for a separator. Because of the size of the window glass base, it is annealed while it cools (see "Fired Glass Decoration"). Very small glass pieces are not annealed.

Some areas of the glass are likely to appear mottled where the enamel has been applied lightly, exposing dots of clear glass. Spray the entire area again, sift with another layer, and fire it a little higher to 1350°F. As you can see, this complex project requires several days for completion although each step is simple and basic.

For the next step, a stencil is laid over the top sky and cottage areas and the lower foreground portion is sifted with purple (a mixture of the red and blue) enamels, fired, and cooled. The enameled window glass base is set aside while stained-glass shapes are cut and fired and the epoxy adhesive is prepared for bonding them.

The original full-scale sketch for this project is traced on stiff paper that is cut into templates. When the stained-glass shapes have been cut out around them, the glass is washed, rinsed, and dried. It is fired on a flat prepared mold to 1300°–1350°F to round the edges. When the glass has cooled, it is carefully rinsed and dried. Remove all particles of kiln wash separator that may cling to it and prevent the epoxy from bonding it.

The lines of the original sketch are emphasized with a felt marker for easy visibility, and it is taped beneath the enameled window glass base as a guide for positioning the fired segments of the stained-glass picture. Each small glass is dabbed with epoxy on its underneath surface, positioned with tweezers, and pressed firmly in place. It is not necessary to spread epoxy over the entire backs of the small pieces. To do so makes them awkward to handle and risks the likelihood of smearing cement over the glass and fingers, which makes a tedious clean-up chore. Fused glass and wire hangers are cemented to the top corners of the glass composition. The completed project must dry undisturbed on a *level* table for several hours. Check it from time to time to make sure the stained glass has not slid out of position, which it can do if the table is not perfectly level.

Embossed glass has exciting potential when it is combined with other glass decorating methods: painting, etching, gilding, and combinations of these and other processes. Its rich colorful quality is well worth the special attention that must be given to sanding or firing the edges of the small shapes and to preparing the special glass epoxy adhesive correctly according to the manufacturer's instructions. A passing gleam of sunshine streaming through the raised bits of colored glass endows even a plain form with wondrous jewellike glamour.

Stained glass scraps are cut up to make small fired "jewels."

The jewels have all sorts of decorative possibilities.

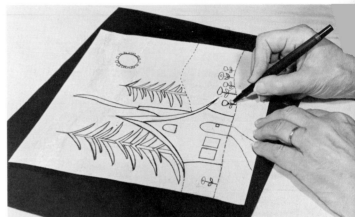

A drawn design is traced over paper toweling for stencils.

A large stencil is wetted and laid on the lower portion of a double-strength window glass panel. The glass base is sprayed with diluted enameling gum; 80-mesh low firing glass enamels are sifted over the exposed sky area.

The glass segments representing tree limbs will be fired to the tree trunk *before* the tree is epoxied to the window glass base. To facilitate transporting them to the flat mold on which they will be fired, they are glued together with Elmer's Glue-All which burns away in the kiln, leaving no ash.

The glued assemblage is easily transported to the firing mold with tweezers.

The fired tree and other shapes are laid out tentatively to plan the composition.

Each stained glass shape is epoxied and pressed into place.

The small cottage is opalescent carmel-and-tan-streaked glass.

Fused Glass Colored with Sifted Enamels

When pieces of glass are fused together, all of them should be cut from the same variety of glass made by the same manufacturer. Because many kinds of materials are used in manufacturing glass, they have different coefficients (degrees) of expansion and contraction in the heat of a kiln. If you are not sure that glasses are of identical composition, test-fire a lamination of small pieces. If they do not fracture upon cooling, you may assume they are similar enough to be compatible.

All the glass to be fused is rinsed and dried. Colored decorating enamels may be sifted over the glass either before or after the pieces are assembled, depending on the desired effect. Dabs of Elmer's Glue-All will hold them in position until they are fused. The glue burns out in the kiln and leaves no ash.

In the illustrated project, a design is drawn and traced on firm paper toweling. Stencils are cut, wetted, and positioned on a clean rectangle of double-strength window glass. The stencils block off clear areas of the glass base where the glass design shapes will be fused, so their colors will not be grayed by the background color. Liquid agar or any commercial enameling gum is diluted, one part gum to three parts water, and sprayed over the entire glass area as an adhesive to hold the glass enamel in place. The enamel is sifted over the background glass around the stencils. Gum is sprayed over all again and the stencils are removed with tweezers. At this point, the glass base can be fired to 1250°F to fuse the background enamel before applied glass shapes are fused to it; or the fusing can take place before any enamels are applied.

In the demonstrated project, however, dabs of Elmer's Glue-All are applied and glass shapes that have been sprayed and sifted with colored enamels are positioned on the unfired enameled base; then the assemblage is given one firing to 1350°F, or until the enamel is shiny and glass edges are rounded. All kilns do not fire alike. Begin checking the progress of the glass at 1250°F. When the firing is completed, the kiln is cooled very slowly because two and three thicknesses of glass are fused. Fast cooling would probably crack the glass. To slow the cooling, turn the kiln on "LOW" from time to time, then turn it off again.

When the glass has cooled completely, remove it from the kiln and wash off any clinging kiln wash. Black decorating color accents are brushed on to sharpen the somewhat pastel glass enamels. Final firing is to 1150° with slow cooling and annealing.

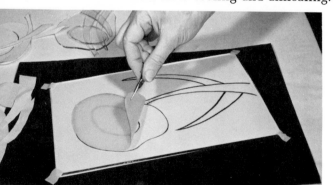

Wet stencils are positioned on the glass base taped over a drawn design.

Turquoise 80-mesh glass enamel is sifted thinly over the background area around the stencils.

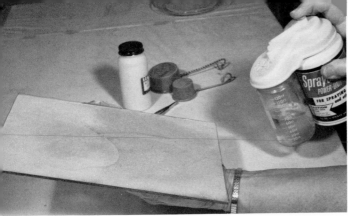

The enameling gum is again sprayed over all.

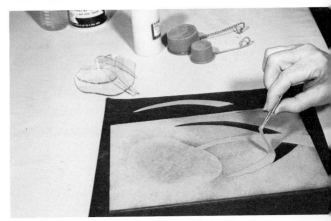

Stencils are carefully picked up and removed with pointed tweezers, revealing the clear spaces where the shapes to be fused will be positioned. The glass panel can be fired at this time, or the enamel-covered glass shapes that will be fused to the bare areas can be positioned and the entire assemblage fused in one firing.

Glass pieces are sprayed and sifted with colored glass enamels.

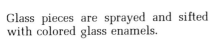

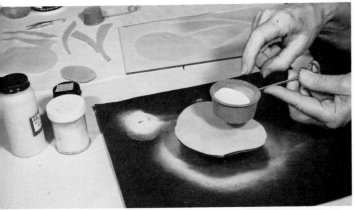

A small stencil is positioned on the flower shape; it is sprayed and sifted with transparent yellow.

It is sprayed again and the stencil is picked off with tweezers.

Elmer's Glue-All is dabbed on the bare glass area to secure the applied shapes while the glass is transported to the kiln.

If you have a steady hand, the enamel-covered shapes can be lowered into place with a small spatula. Take care that unfired background colors are not disturbed. The background glass can be fired separately, and the applied shapes are positioned more easily with dabs of glue holding them secure as shown in the illustration.

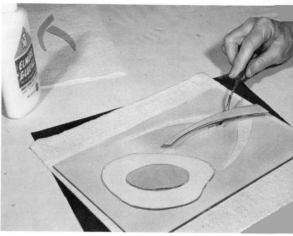

Everything is in readiness to go into the kiln on a shelf that has been given a coating of kiln wash. It may be easier to position the assemblage on the kiln shelf outside the kiln, then insert the shelf and glass together into the kiln.

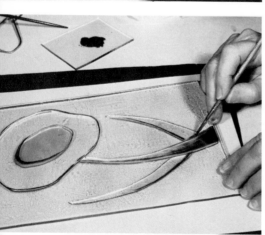

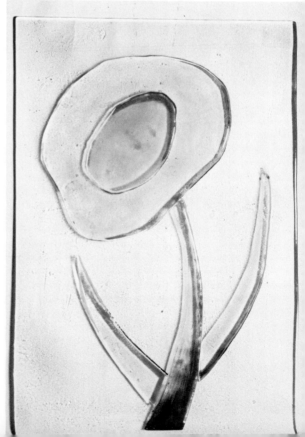

Black glass decorating color is brushed in a few places to accent the pastel glass colors. It is fired to 1150°F.

Fused glass in turquoise, yellow, brown, and aqua.

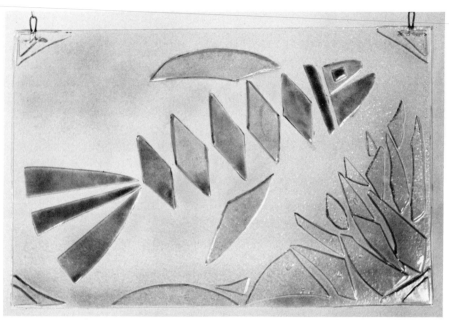

Individual glass pieces that make up the fish were enameled and fired separately. They were then adhered to the glass base with glue. The clear glass seaweed shapes and corners on the glass (including wire hangers) were not prefired. Colors were sifted over all except the fish. Firing was 1400°. The glue burns out in the kiln.

GLASS LANDSCAPE. Clear glass was fused, then colored and fired again.

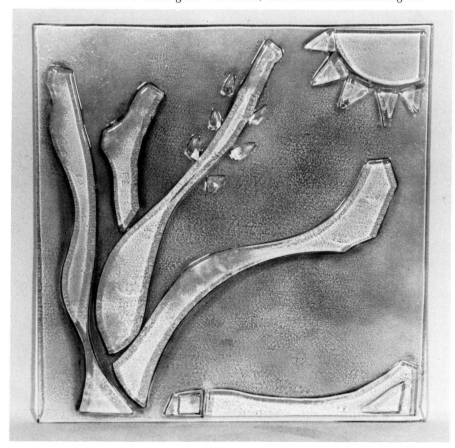

Embossing by Fired Indentation over Wire and Other Materials

Single-strength or double-strength window glass or sheet stained glass bends and takes on the contours of metal or clay objects when it is fired over them in a kiln. A "separator" must be applied to the kiln shelf (or other firing base) and to the object over which the glass is bent, to prevent the glass from sticking to them at the temperature required to slump the glass. The separator used for projects in this book is kiln wash, either powdered and sifted or mixed with water for brushing. It is available at ceramic supply stores. Whiting (calcium carbonate) is another possible separator. Once they have been used for a separator, these materials should not be employed for other purposes. The glass to be bent or embossed is cut at least an inch wider than the outermost limits of the object over which it will slump to allow some glass to flatten out around the perimeter of the composition. Avoid any objects that have undercut areas. When glass is contoured in the kiln, it becomes quite pliant; it will slump closely over the object beneath it. After it cools and the glass hardens, it cannot be lifted off the object if there are any undercuts in it.

If wire is the contouring object, spaces of half an inch or more must be allowed between wires to permit the glass to settle between them. Copper, brass, or nichrome wires are suitable. The wire should be at least 12 gauge if you would have a dynamic subsurface indentation. Thinner wire of 14 or 16 gauge combines well with heavier wire for interesting variation. It is doubtful whether wire of thinner than 16 gauge will show much indentation in the glass, especially if it is double-strength window glass. Bend the wire with your fingers whenever possible. If necessary, draw a guiding line pattern of your idea and check it from time to time by laying the wire over it. If the wire should stiffen suddenly while you are working it, heat it with a torch or in a kiln until it is red hot, then pick it up with firing tongs and plunge it into water. This process is called "annealing metal." It is a different process from annealing glass. Annealing metal restores its malleability so it is easily worked again. To remove fire scale that has formed on the wire when it is annealed, soak it in a Sparex II solution. Sparex is sold in most ceramic supply stores. Follow the printed directions on the container. Where one wire crosses another in the design, cut the top wire, then continue a piece of it from the opposite side of the "crossed" wire. Although the wires will then lie flat against the base surface, they will appear to cross. If they should actually be crossed and form a hump in the wire, the glass may slide off it in the kiln.

The demonstrated project begins with a 7" circle of PPG single-strength window glass and 12-gauge copper wire. The glass is washed and dried. It can be colored on the top surface before it is embossed. Metal enamels will not fuse satisfactorily to glass because of the difference in their coefficients of expansion in the heat of the kiln. A small amount of bright-colored copper enamel can be blended with high-fire glass enamel (seven parts glass enamel to one part copper enamel), however, to deepen the more pastel glass enamel color. Spray the glass with enameling gum and sift a thin layer of enamel over it. Spray again and sift another thin layer twice more. Let it dry completely and fire it to 1425°F on a kiln shelf covered with kiln wash or whiting for a separator. Let the kiln cool naturally with the door closed tightly.

For the project at hand, the 12-gauge copper wire is bent in a simple hand-formed nonrepresentational design of two parts. The completed design is bent, tapped, and pressed until it will lie flat on the kiln shelf. Any portion that remains raised above the kiln shelf may flex in the heat of the kiln and cause the glass to slide from its position on top of the wire. When the wire design is completed, a thin coating of separator is brushed over it as smoothly as possible. It is dried and positioned with care on the prepared kiln shelf. If it has been annealed, it will be very pliant and easily distorted, so handle it gingerly. In the demonstrated project, the enamel is sifted on the glass and fired over the bent wire in *one* firing.

Twelve-gauge copper wire is bent in a simple design. It is brushed with a solution of kiln wash and water.

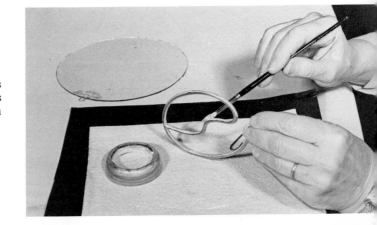

Enamel is sifted over the glass and a small tab of glass laid on top of a bent wire hanger.

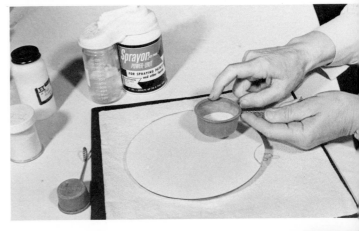

The wire design is positioned on the kiln shelf.

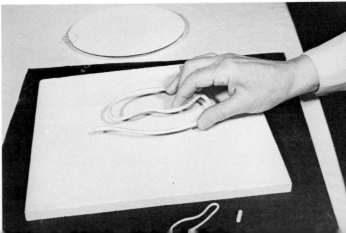

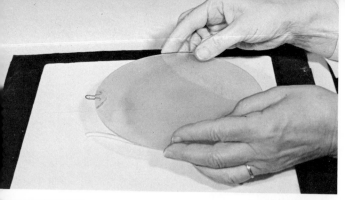

The prepared circle of glass is placed on top of the wire design.

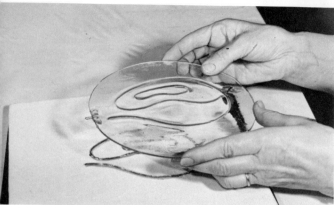

When the glass has been fired and cooled, the indented glass is lifted off the wire.

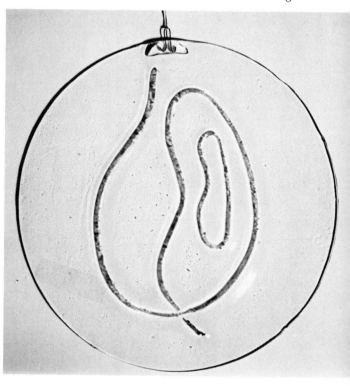

Subsurface indentation. Light-colored stained glass can be indented instead of enameled window glass.

Embossing over Clay

Glass can be indented over a modeled clay design that has been fired in the kiln, but *not glazed.* The thickness and viscosity of the glass as it fires prevents duplication of fine details; consequently simple designs boldly modeled or deeply indented in the clay are more effective than elaborate shallow patterning. To make one of these clay molds, use ready-prepared white ungrogged sculpture clay bought directly from your ceramic supplier and available in 5- to 50-pound plastic bags. Roll out some of the clay about an inch larger all around than your planned relief design. Clay shrinks when it dries and when it is fired. Let it dry until it is firm but not stiff. In this condition, it is easily carved in relief. A bold design with a few widely spaced lines is deeply cut and modeled. Avoid making any undercuts in the clay.

If you are making a relief panel such as the one illustrated, lay the completed panel on several sheets of newspaper on a board or table, cover it with an equal number of newssheets, and place a thin board on top of the papers; avoid pressing down on it because to do so may tend to flatten your carefully wrought design. The newspapers and board will keep the panel from warping as it dries.

Several small holes must be drilled through a clay mold wherever air can be trapped as the glass slumps. Otherwise large bubbles will form in the glass as it softens. It is far easier to drill through unfired dry clay than through fired clay, although care must be taken to avoid cracking the mold. Do not use an electric drill. Use a hand drill and do not press against the clay but let the weight of the drill carry it down. The holes can be drilled safely through fired clay, but hard silica in the clay will use up the small bits rapidly. The illustrated clay mold was drilled before it was fired.

The sculpture clay was fired to cone 08 (1800°F), which leaves the clay essentially porous and less likely to crack when glass is fired over it. Fire it on several clay stilts to prevent it from warping in the heat of the kiln. The fired clay mold is cooled and brushed with a *thin solution* of kiln wash and water, which prevents the glass from sticking to it when it is bent in the kiln. Before you apply the kiln wash, if you plunge the mold into water and quickly withdraw it, you will find that the wash will cover the mold smoothly and easily. This operation makes the mold quite wet; it must be dried completely for at least 24 hours, before the glass is bent over it to 1400°–1450°F. Begin checking the progress of the glass at 1350°. Open the door just far enough to see that the glass is settling into its mold, then quickly close it. Let the kiln cool naturally. The demonstration panel of yellow stained glass is not given additional decoration.

If the worktable is near the kiln, the project will not be transported very far and is less likely to be disarranged while in transit. With Elmer's Glue-All, adhere a small piece of glass over a nichrome wire loop to the edge of the glass circle for a hanger. It will fuse to the glass while it slumps over the wire. The prepared circle of glass is lowered gently on top of the wire and the assemblage is inserted into the kiln. When all are in place, it is time to turn on the kiln switch. The kiln door is left ajar about 1/4" and the switch is turned to "LOW" until the pyrometer indicates at least 450°F. It may take two hours or longer, depending on the room temperature and the quantity of glass being fired. AT 450°F, the switch is turned to "HIGH." At 950° the door is closed tightly. It is advisable at this point to *stay near the kiln.* With the switch on high and the door closed, the temperature will rise rapidly. The illustrated embossed project is fired to 1425°, which repeated firings have shown to be the ideal top firing temperature for this process. A kiln should be tested with sample firings, however, because kilns do not all heat the same way; begin checking the temperature at 1350° to see whether the glass is settling over the wires. If all looks as planned, the kiln switch is turned off at 1425°F and the door is opened a crack for a few moments to halt the temperature rise from heat stored in the kiln walls. Then the door is closed again. When the pyrometer shows the temperature has dropped to 1000°F, the switch is turned on again to "LOW" to hold the temperature between 900° and 1000° for a heat-soaking period of an hour that will anneal the glass and remove strain that could make it brittle. After that time, the kiln switch is turned off and left to cool naturally, preferably overnight. If you form the habit of annealing your fired glass, you will probably never have glass breakage from carefully handled fired glass projects. Subsurface indented embossed glass is one more interesting glass decorative method that can be combined with other processes or developed into a complex project of several units to transmit or reflect gleaming rays of light.

A bold design is traced firmly over the slab of moist firm clay. The design will be scored, cut, and modeled.

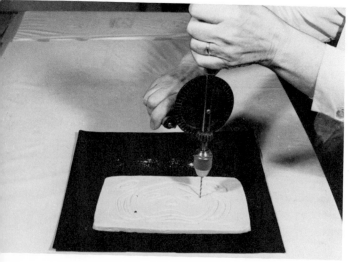

Small holes are drilled through the dried clay. Drilling is gentle and careful to avoid cracking the clay. Holes permit air to escape when glass is slumped over the mold; otherwise trapped air would gather in big unwanted bubbles of glass.

The clay is fired on small stilts to allow heat to circulate in the kiln and prevent warpage.

The fired clay is brushed with a thin solution of kiln wash and water. Plunge the mold quickly into and out of water *before* kiln wash is applied, for smooth, easy brushing.

Light yellow antique stained glass.

4

* Engraving
and Etching
Glass

The Vibrating Engraver

There are several kinds of engraving tools and methods for engraving on glass: (1) A *vibrating engraver* is a small hand-held electric tool with a fine carborundum point or a diamond point that vibrates up and down approximately 7200 strokes per minute. It makes very minute frosted white dots in the glass, which form delicate lines when it is moved over the glass surface like a pencil. This fascinating method creates frosted white patterns that are most effective on clear transparent glass. (2) *Drill* engraving is another method that originated with modern small hand-held electric tools. Artist-craftsmen, ever alert to make use of new tools, processes, and materials, were quick to adapt this tool to their needs. The tool is especially useful for grinding and clearing away the top color layer of flashed glass to leave a shallow relief design of shining stained glass set in a background of the matt white glass layer beneath it. The tool can also engrave line and stipple effects with various bits that revolve in a metal holder attached to the electric hand drill or in a flexible shaft attached to a spindle of a stationary motor. (3) *Copper wheel* engraving is the grinding away of the glass in patterns by the use of small copper wheels working over a mixture of light oil and abrasive grains (400 to 600 mesh). The glass is brought up to the wheel and is moved against it, unlike the first two methods discussed here in which the engraving tool moves over the glass. Copper tool engraving has a light sheen over its frosted effect. (4) *Diamond point* engraving with a stylus-type graver combines lines and small dot stippling in a delicate, almost invisible effect. The outline of the design is engraved; then it is filled in by tapping fine dots (stipple) or by engraving parallel lines laid close together, or both.

Copper wheel and diamond point engraving require considerable skill and practice. After experience with the two methods demonstrated here, it may be very rewarding for the budding glass engraver to investigate copper wheel and diamond point techniques. The first tool demonstrated is the *vibrating engraver.*

It is advisable to practice on whatever glass is available to you such as thin picture glass or scraps of single-strength window glass, if it is not too hard. If a tool does not mark easily on glass, it may be that it is too hard; search for a softer glass that does not dull your tool. When you progress to three-dimensional objects, try a plain tumbler or drinking glass with straight sides and test its response to the graver. Even a very light tinted glass, which produces white lines under the graver point, can give some attractive results.

To begin, draw on paper a simple suitable design made of many lines and a few shaded areas. The design can be drawn on black paper with a white chalk pencil or in ink on white paper. Tape the drawing under flat glass with extra paper extending beyond the glass so it can be turned as work progresses. The design can be cut directly into the glass with the engraver by following the drawn lines beneath the glass; or it can be traced onto the glass with a white graphite pencil and the engraving done on top of this white tracing. In this case, plain black paper is placed under the glass so the work is seen easily. Some engravers find the white drawn lines tend to obscure the white engraved lines. Both methods can be tried to determine which works best for you. When you are working on glass with a vibrating or grinding tool, *wear a protective nose mask* so you do not breathe glass dust. The masks are sold in most drugstores and they are inexpensive.

Our first demonstrated project is engraved with a vibrating engraver that has calibrated adjustable stroke lengths. For work on glass, use the strokes (lowest setting) *that produce engraving visible enough* to meet the

Three drawings for the first engraving design.

Engraving strokes are practiced separately with the vibrating engraver and scrap glass. A glass piece is taped over the drawn pattern. Hold the engraving tool like a pencil, tilting it *slightly* toward you. The tool setting for matting in # 1½.

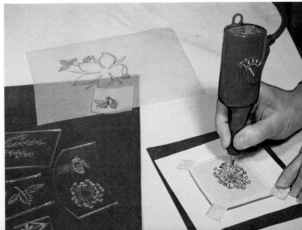

A nine-inch circle of double-strength crystal glass with a polished edge is taped over the main pattern. Brace the engraving hand very firmly against the table; the tool's point is traced carefully and lightly along the glass above the line drawing under it. Tool setting for outlining is # 2.

needs of your design plan for light shading or deeper effects. Experiment with different settings by trying them on scrap glass. The carbide steel engraving point that is often furnished with the tool is removable; replacement points may be ordered from the tool's manufacturer.

For our project, after practicing on picture glass, a circle of lovely crystal glass is taped over a pattern of black lines on white paper. To avoid annoying light spots, the work light is adjusted so it does not reflect on the glass. When you work with a vibrating engraver, support your hand on the table and hold the tool firmly while you press the engraver point very lightly on the glass and move it along over the drawn lines. Turn the drawing as you work so the angle at which your hand must move the tool, to follow the lines of your guiding sketch, is natural and comfortable. Move the graver deliberately so you may achieve fine work; errors cannot be erased! Before you start on an ambitious project, it is advisable to practice on scrap picture glass the actual strokes you will be using on the project design itself such as the curves, straight lines, circles, and dots, until you can make smooth marks with even cutting depth.

The illustrated project involves several steps that develop different problems. Beginning with a simple engraved flower and leaves, a second part of the design, consisting of the stamens, *is laid over it.* There are long graceful curves and many short lines. Parts of the outlined areas are filled in with matting achieved by laying delicate short strokes close together. The small flying bee is engraved with very light strokes and stippled areas. To produce fine lines, the engraver is held nearly vertical and is applied to the glass with a very light touch. For matting broad areas, it is slanted like a pencil and many lines are laid close together. To stipple, touch the engraver's point to the glass to make small dotted areas. When you finish a project like this, you will feel like a professional although the individual parts of the design are basic.

Matting for filling in the stamens is engraved in thin parallel lines set closely together. Setting is # 1½. The pattern for the stamens is laid under the glass as a guide for the overlay design.

Completed glass insert for a small tabletop. The glass is installed in reverse so the top surface is absolutely smooth. A set of these engraved circles with delicate engraving can also make elegant place mats on a medium or dark colored tabletop.

Engraving Three-Dimensional Glass

Engraving on a curved glass surface presents problems that are not encountered when flat glass is engraved. (1) The curvature of the surface tends to slightly distort the lines of the guiding sketch under the glass. This distortion must be taken into account as the engraving tool is moved over the glass above these lines. If you move the tool slowly and deliberately with close attention paid to the direction of the lines, you should have little difficulty. (2) For your first efforts to engrave on three-dimensional glass, it is advisable to avoid engraving near the thicker base of a piece, found on most glassware. The lines of a design on the pattern behind thick glass are difficult to follow because they are separated from the tip of the engraving tool by this extra thickness. At first you may tend to strike the glass sooner than you expect as you lower the tool toward it. (3) Another problem to deal with is that of fitting a drawn pattern to the inside of the glass so a surplus amount of folded paper does not conceal some parts of the sketch. To alleviate this problem, after the design is drawn, cut closely around it to remove all excess paper. There is no practical reason why a paper pattern for engraving must be kept in a rectangular or square form. Cut away the excess paper, leaving enough of it to hold the design together and to allow tabs of masking tape to fasten it inside the glass.

It is advisable to begin with a simple design. It should fit easily into the space allotted for it. Placement and size of the design are important. It should be large enough to have vitality, yet not appear crowded. Too

The paper pattern guide for engraving on a three-dimensional glass is cut closely around the design to eliminate the need for making slits and folds in surplus paper. It is taped against the inside of the glass.

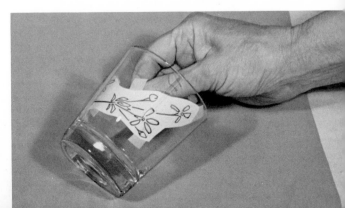

small a design may look insignificant, regardless of the excellence of its technique. It is well to leave at least a half-inch space between the design and the top of the glass, unless the subject is very small. Remember to keep the engraving above the thickness at the base of the glass.

Practice and work out your problems on an inexpensive glass or other expendable subject before you apply the engraving tool to a cherished glass object. If a first three-dimensional subject for engraving is a straight-sided piece such as the demonstrated glass, you will feel less nervous when the engraving tool makes its first mark than you might with a valuable crystal goblet. This relaxed calmness itself can almost assure your success. Should you make an unsightly error, you can discard the glass with little loss; but you will have gained valuable experience.

Before you begin work, anchor the glass in some way so it does not slip while you are engraving. It can be pressed into a small sandbag or against the worktable top. When you have completed the simple outlining, remove the pattern from the glass and position the glass on a black surface so the more detailed engraving is easily seen. Continue engraving the stippling with tiny dots and the matting with closely spaced parallel lines just as you did on flat glass.

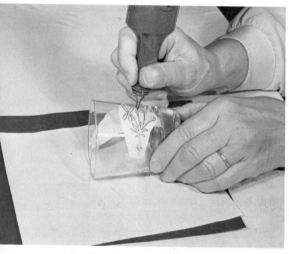

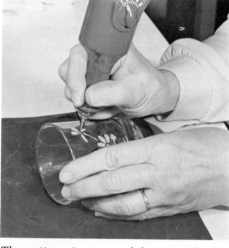

Outlines are engraved on the glass over the pattern beneath it. The right hand presses firmly against the table; the left hand holds the glass secure.

The pattern is removed from inside the glass. Hold the glass firmly against a black background surface while the tool is engraving lightly but consistently and with care. Parallel lines are engraved closely together to mat fill-in areas. Set the tool at 1½ for matting.

Completed engraving on an old-fashioned glass.

Antique frosted glass vase, enameled and gilded. *Collection of the author.*

ANGEL FISH. Polly Rothenberg. Stained glass painting with bonded glass "jewels."

Engraved flashed stained glass. Fredrica Fields.

Canister gilded and embossed with stained glass. Decorated by Polly Rothenberg.

Reverse painting under glass above a
mirror. Polly Rothenberg.

SUN MOUNTAIN. Laura Popenoe.
Glass mosaic tabletop with antique and
gold glass tesserae, tiles, stones, shells.
*Courtesy Rosey Juniper Studio,
California.*

BURNING BUSH. Laura Popenoe. Mirrored stained glass and gold glass.

DARK ANGEL. Laura Popenoe. Mirrored stained glass mosaic sculpture.

Hand-painted decoration, unfired. Polly Rothenberg.

CITY SCENE. Wilma Cymbala. Painted glass, unfired.

Hand-painted amber glass goblet, unfired. Decorated by Wilma Cymbala.

Venetian goblet. Angelo
Beroviero (c. 1475). Enamel
and gilt. *Courtesy of the
Toledo Museum of Art; gift
of Edward Drummond
Libbey.*

MOON FACE and SUN
FACE medallions flanking
FULL-RIGGED SHIP
triptych, painted glass. Glass
Masters Guild.

BUTTERFLIES. Polly Rothenberg. Painted and gilded stained glass panel on a plastic easel.

COTTAGE RETREAT. Polly Rothenberg. Fired stained glass shapes cemented to enameled sheet glass.

MORNING SUN. Beth Beede. Enameled fused glass with wire, beads, and dyed wool.

Stained glass medallion. Polly Rothenberg. Painted, sgraffitoed, and fired.

ROAD RUNNER, CLOWN OF THE WEST. Polly Rothenberg. Bonded antique glass on clear sheet, unfired.

BIRDS. Fredrica Fields.
Engraved flashed glass
medallion.

Engraved and leaded stained
glass. Fredrica Fields.

Engraving on Flashed Glass, Narrated by Fredrica Fields

The variety of antique stained glass known as "flashed" glass has a light-colored base layer topped with a thin skin of rich, deeper, contrasting colored glass. When a pattern in one of these glass layers is created by etching, engraving, or sandblasting, mingled glints of light and color shine through to delight the eye. Fredrica Fields, eminent professional glass artist of Greenwich, Connecticut, describes in detail her expertise in engraving this color-layered antique flashed glass:

A new way to cut through the "flashed" layer became possible with the development of the small portable power drill and the many abrasive bits usable on glass. Little danger is involved. Protection for the eyes and a lightweight mask over the nose and mouth are advisable because of the fine dust this dry grinding process creates ... the edge of the design should be clean-cut and accurate.

To prepare for engraving on flashed glass, a shallow light-box with an opaque (opal) glass surface is set in or on a table of convenient height. Two fluorescent bulbs set fairly close together under the opal glass give sufficient light. A comfortable straight-backed chair, preferably with easy-rolling casters, should be at a height to permit the knees to go under the light-box. One or more of the small power drills and a selection of grinding bits for glass comprise the essential equipment needed. The constant speed of these drills is right for the work. (Manufacturers of the tools are Handee and Dremel.)

As a guide, a carefully developed drawing on transparent paper or Mylar is used. The drawing is inked in as black as possible, and it is protected by a clear acetate slipcase. In preparing a design, it should be remembered that the desired result is a flat figure in sharp silhouette, one color contrasting against the other.

The glass to be worked, precut for the specific design, and with the "flashed" side up, is taped to the drawing with masking tape. This prevents any slippage out of position, and also protects the bottom side of the glass from the scratches that might occur as it is moved about during the engraving process. A small brush at hand is useful to keep the fine grit off the table and the work. The design can be engraved directly on the glass with the drawing under it.

GAZELLE BOWL. Steuben Glass Company, Corning, New York. Heavy glass bowl with cut and engraved pattern of gazelles. *Photo by courtesy of The Toledo Museum of Art. Gift of William E. Levis.*

There are two main types of grinding bits for glass: the flat disk and the cone and cylinder. A great deal of fast work can be done with the flat disk, called the cut-off or separating disk. It can also do a great deal of damage rapidly, and can chip shallow "flashes" easily. The cone and cylinder type bits are shaped against a shaping stone and do very delicate work as well as coarse work, grinding away the "flash" little by little. Cone and cylinder bits of several diameters and lengths are needed. (Available from Handee, Dremel, or Foredom companies; cut-off disks carried by dental suppliers.)

Two hand positions are involved. The cut-off disk requires the drill to be held horizontal to the table. The eye observes the grinding from behind the disk at an angle. This creates a distortion of the drawing if not taken into account; keeping the disk *well inside* the line of the drawing compensates for the error. The cone and cylinder bits require that the drill be held more upright in the hand, as though for writing position. To follow the drawing correctly with these bits, the head must be held as directly over the bit as possible. It is wise to engrave a little inside the line throughout the work thus leaving some area of glass for later correction or improvement.

Firm control of the drill is necessary so the abrasive bit stays in place. If the cone or cylinder bit is not kept aligned with the work and leans sideways, it is likely to roll suddenly across the glass and out of the design area, leaving a mark. To prevent this, it is necessary to move the drawing constantly so that the angle of the bit is always correct. If these bits are urged along more rapidly than they are clearing the "flash" away, the same thing may occur. Should the artist bear down too heavily this will cause a deeper gouge that looks unsightly and renders the spot difficult to improve if the line is not satisfactory. The cut-off disk is worked from left to right and right to left and will overrun the edge of the design if not stopped in time. The texture created by the many short strokes of these abrasive bits adds considerable interest to the work.

The engraving completed, the glass is fired in a kiln in the same manner as painted stained-glass work. The firing removes the whitish surface the dry grinding points create and restores a glassy look to the engraved area. It softens the sharp edges of the "flashed" layer where engraving has taken place. The visibility of any light scratches that may have occurred by the bit rolling out of control is lessened. The tempera-

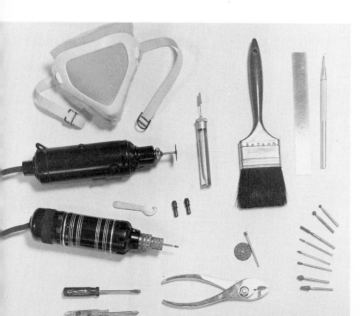

Basic tools for engraving glass.

ture similar to that required for the firing of pigment is satisfactory ... the perfect firing spot in the kiln is found through experimentation with discarded pieces of flashed glass. After it is fired the glass piece is leaded or framed for display in a window.

This method of engraving is appealing and challenging. Its great appeal is that one is always dealing with color. The challenge lies in the difficulties inherent in the method and the material ... and yet, when the completed piece is removed from the kiln, shining in its glassy beauty, and is held up to the light, there is a thrill and satisfaction that sends one back to the drawing board and the light table. As expertise is acquired, many of the problems decrease. Each undertaking is a new adventure.

Fredrica Fields engraving over a light box. *Photos by Kenneth E. Fields.*

Black ink drawing on transparent paper. The edges are reinforced with masking tape before the drawing is slipped into a clear acetate cover to keep out dust and grit.

The circle of flashed glass is laid on the drawing and is taped to it securely with masking tape.

Hand position for engraving with cone and cylinder bits.

The hand position employed for engraving with the cutoff disc.

Etching with Special Cream

It is advisable to make a trial effort on a piece of flat window glass before you attempt to etch a choice glass object. An etched design error on glass cannot be successfully erased or covered. After you achieve a satisfactory sample etching project, select a simple shape such as a saucer, plate, or small panel before you begin a more elaborate design. Wash the glass in hot detergent water to remove all soil and finger marks. Rinse it in warm water and dry it completely. Hold the clean glass by its edges to keep it clean. Set it aside with a cover to protect it from dust while you prepare the design and materials for etching.

The special etching cream is available in small and large tubes. It is effective and easy to apply when the manufacturer's instructions are followed in detail.* Hydrofluoric acid employed by large professional glass studios for etching glass designs presents hazards for the novice craftsman and for the beginner who is working without expert supervision and adequate ventilation. Stencils for etching glass are made of a special adhesive aluminum design foil, usually obtainable where the etching cream is sold. Both positive and negative stencils are useful in this technique.

Trace or draw on tracing paper a design that suits the space and shape to be decorated. The design for an initial project should be simple and easy to cut out for a stencil. Cut a piece of the adhesive-backed foil, allowing plenty of margin around the area that will be filled by the planned design. With a bluntly pointed pencil, retrace your design onto the foil, applying

*See "Supply Sources."

firm, even pressure. Follow the indented lines and carefully cut out the stencil with small sharp *pointed* scissors that will begin the cut without making a ragged hole. With a pair of tweezers, hold the dull side of the cut foil stencil close to a mild dry heat source, such as a lighted lamp bulb or a candle, to activate the foil's adhesive backing until it is tacky but *not sticky.* Then press the warm stencil against the glass object in its planned position. Roll a smooth round pencil or small dowel stick over it on flat glass. On curved glass surfaces, press it down by stroking it with the back of a small, smooth, plastic spoon until all edges are firmly adhered to the glass. The edges can be pressed down further with the back of a fingernail. Should the etching cream seep under a loose edge, it will make a ragged uneven finish.

For the illustrated project, the etching cream is spread generously and smoothly over the exposed design area with a Q-Tip cotton swab dabbed gently over the exposed glass within the design area. Any tiny air bubbles are patted away. After at least three minutes or longer, the cream is activated and has etched the glass; no harm is done if it is left on longer. To make an even etching, a second coating of the cream must be applied. The first application is removed with *cold water* before the second one is applied. Do not let the full force of the faucet water run directly against the foil or it will surely loosen the stencil. Hold a wad of soft cotton between the stream of water and the stencil, while you gently swab off the etching cream. As a further precaution against loosening the stencil, you may even let the force of the water flow against the back of your hand and down over the cotton as it swabs away the cream. Pat the glass dry with a paper towel and apply a *second coat* of etching cream. Because of its jellylike consistency, it is patted and pushed to cover the glass within the design area. After three or more minutes, rinse off the cream and the foil stencil with plenty of hot water. If you have followed all directions carefully, you will find you have created a truly delicate and lovely ornamental glass object.

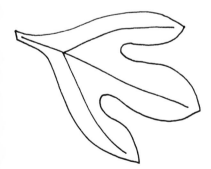

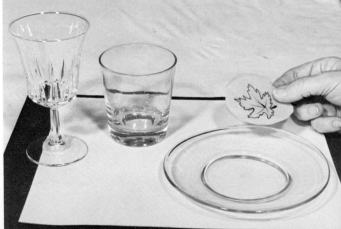

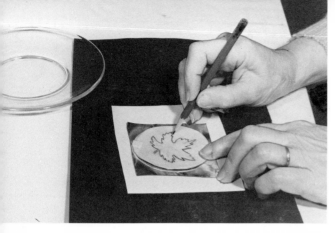

A bluntly pointed pencil is traced firmly over the leaf outline to transfer the design to the special adhesive-backed etching foil.

The foil pattern is cut out and adhered to the back of the plate. Etching cream is applied with a cotton-tipped swab to cover the open glass area within the stencil cutout.

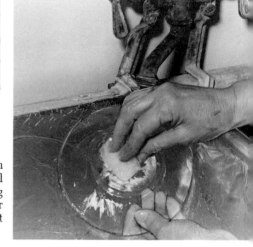

After three minutes, hold a wad of cotton between the stream of water and the stencil while you gently swab off the etching cream. Do not let the full force of the water run directly on the foil, if you do not want the foil loosened.

The delicately etched plate.

The tracing paper pattern has vertical cuts along the lower edge to fit it into the glass. Etching foil stencil is cut into three manageable sections.

Press the back of a plastic spoon against cut edges of the foil stencil to adhere them snugly against the glass.

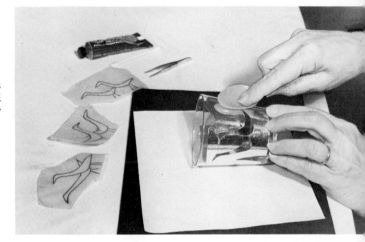

Pat etching cream over the stencil opening with a small cotton swab where the glass is exposed. After three minutes, gently rinse it off.

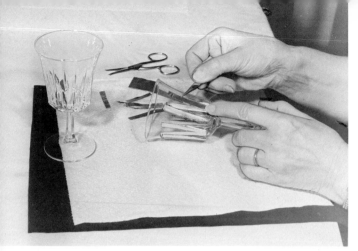

On the goblet, indented triangular areas are blocked off with strips of adhesive foil.

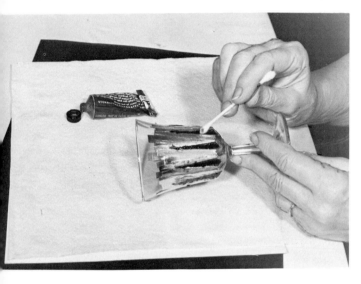

Etching cream is patted on the open triangular areas for three minutes. Regular procedure is followed.

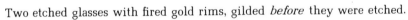

Two etched glasses with fired gold rims, gilded *before* they were etched.

5

* Glass Jewelry

Macramé and glass collar with clear glass pendant laminated with transparent pink enamel and silver wire. By Bette Warner.

Lamination and Surface Decoration

The decorative techniques discussed so far are adaptable in miniature to making delightful jewelry, either in stained glass or clear sheet glass. An effective and unusual glass decorating method, especially suitable for jewelry, is the fusing together of two or more layers of glass, entrapping between them design materials that could not be successfully fired to the top glass surface. Due to the differences in their coefficients of expansion and contraction when subjected to the heat of a kiln, such materials tend to crack loose or scale off the surface after they are fired and cooled. For example, *enamels* that are made *for firing on metals are not usually compatible with glass;* but they are available in more and brighter colors than glass enamels. They can be fired successfully between identical glass layers to 1500°F. Seen through the glass, the sandwiched colors have unusual depth and beauty.

Flattened silver wire designs, underglazes, and some other materials are also safely fused and laminated between layers of clean identical glass. Small bubbles that sometimes form around these entrapped designs can be quite decorative. Silver or nichrome wire loops laminated between glass layers at the edge of jewelry shapes give them great versatility as hangers (or jump rings) for pendants and connectors of units for bracelets and necklaces. In addition, wire is effective for making decorative designs between glass layers. When fine silver wire is fired between light-colored stained glass, it sometimes changes color, although in general it retains

81

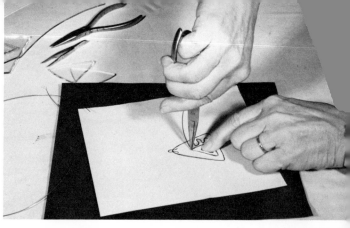

Fine silver wire is bent with jewelry pliers by following a line drawing for a laminated design. Wire is 20-gauge.

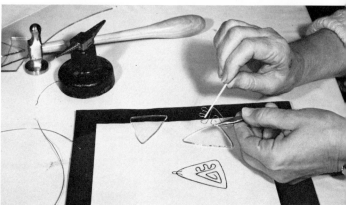

After the wire design is pounded flat, dabs of Elmer's Glue-All are applied to it; the glue burns out in the kiln and leaves no ash. The wire is adhered on a triangle of single-strength window glass.

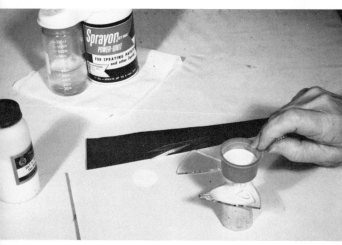

Enameling gum is sprayed over the assemblage and transparent metal enamel is sifted generously over all.

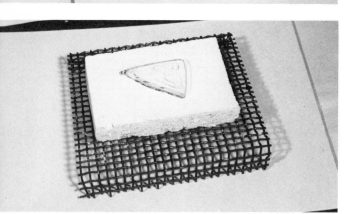

A wire loop and a second glass piece are positioned over the first glass. The pendant is positioned on insulation brick that is rubbed with dry kiln wash for a separator. Firing is to 1450°F to fuse the glass and enamel.

The completed pendant. Tiny bubbles around the wires give added interest.

Wire and yellow enamel lamination between clear glass layers.

Bracelet of polished rosewood and yellow stained glass with laminated wire. A single strand of 18-gauge fine silver wire forms end loops and a laminated design in each glass link. Fire to 1375°F.

its clean silver color. The metallic coloring oxides in some glasses or in some powdered glass decorating colors may turn the silver to gold (pink is one such glass color). Fine silver may turn to a rich copper color when it is combined with yellow glass or coloring agents when fired. *Sterling* silver and nichrome wires turn gray if they are fired to glass. Any of the wires, usually in 18 to 22 guage, should be pounded and flattened, and if used for hanging, loops should be twisted double, then flattened, before lamination.

Pairs of identical small clear glass jewelry squares, rectangles, or other shapes that have brightly colored enamels and wire suspension loops laminated between them form the base for any kind of surface glass jewelry decoration. In addition, scraps and bits of colorful flat or chunk stained glass can be melted into small jewels, tumbled in a lapidary tumbler, gilded, and epoxied to clear or stained glass as well as to other materials for imaginative and fashionable objects of personal adornment.

Paper towel stencil strips are dipped in water (so they lie flat) and positioned on a glass shape.

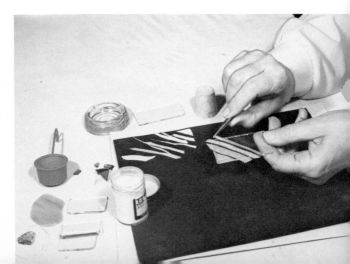

Enameling gum adhesive is sprayed and opalescent white glass enamel is sifted over all.

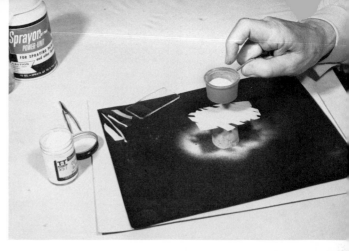

Each stencil strip of paper is lifted off carefully with tweezers.

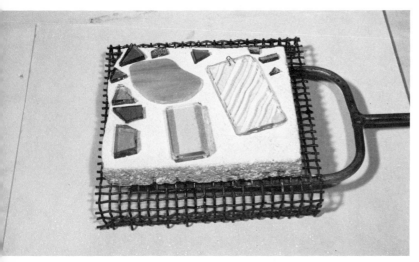

A second glass rectangle and a wire loop are placed on top of the first glass. The assemblage and several miscellaneous glass shapes are placed on a mold and fired to 1450°F.

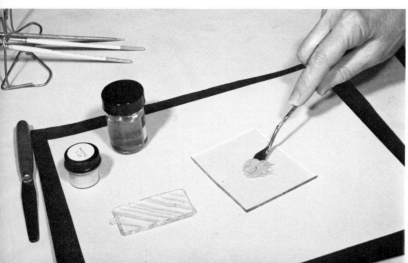

Glass decorating powder is blended with squeegee oil to make a paint mixture.

Stripes are applied in yellow paint.

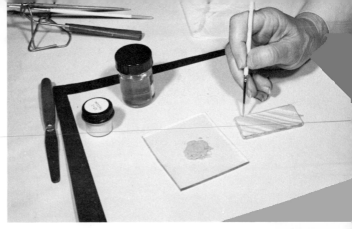

Black decorating powder is blended for final stripes. They are dried and fired to 1100°F to just fuse the paint.

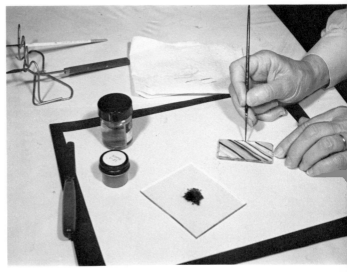

Completed pendant with laminated white opal stripes and painted surface stripes for an interesting effect.

Scraps of single-strength window glass are glued together, sprayed with enameling adhesive and sifted with transparent blue glass enamel. Firing is 1450°F to fuse the glass.

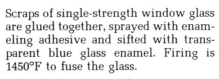

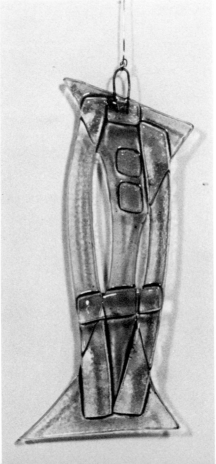

Pairs of identical glass shapes are brushed with squeegee oil or enameling gum and sifted with colored transparent enamel.

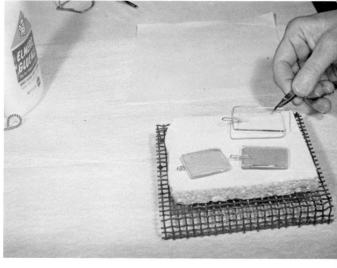

Wire loops are glued under a second glass; it is placed on an enamel-covered glass for lamination at 1450°F.

Laminated pendants with surface decoration; *left,* engraving and gilt; *center,* embossed stained glass; *right,* fired enamel.

* *Glossary*

(This glossary is intended for quick reference; refer to index and text for detailed explanations.)

Aerosol Sprayer. Contains gas under compression; used for power spraying of liquids to give a fine spray mist.

Aluminum Design Foil. An adhesive-backed foil made especially for cutting out positive and negative stencils.

Annealing Glass. The heating and slow cooling of glass to relieve stress and brittleness. The temperature range for annealing varies, depending on the composition of the glass.

Annealing Metal. Making metal malleable by subjecting it to high heat and fast cooling.

Antique Glass. Stained glass made from blowing glass. Varying thicknesses and textures are typical of this glass.

Banding Wheel. A round flat disk that is revolved by hand on a fixed base.

Bonded. Glass pieces that have been adhered to a glass base with epoxy adhesive.

Bridge. A flat board elevated on subsurface end blocks. It supports the hand above glass that is being painted.

Bubble. Air pocket trapped in glass when it is made or when it is fused.

Carborundum Paper. An abrasive paper for sanding sharp edges off glass under water.

Cathedral Glass. Machine-rolled stained glass with medium to heavy texture on one side and smooth on the other side. It is of 1/8" uniform thickness.

Circle Cutter. A glass cutter with a pivoting arm that holds the cutting wheel. It is employed for cutting out circles of glass.

Coefficients of Expansion. The rate at which glass and other materials expand when heated and contract when cooled.

Crystal Glass. Glass of exceptional clarity and brilliance.

Cutting Glass. Scoring glass preparatory to effecting separation along the scored line by tapping or bending it down over the table edge.

Double-Strength Glass. Window glass of 1/8" thickness.

Easel. A support for holding flat glass in a nearly perpendicular position.

Embossed. Having a raised decorative design.

Enamel. A fired vitreous paint. Granular enamels are sifted over an adhesive; powdered enamels are mixed with a medium and brushed on the glass before they are fired in a kiln.

Engraving. Incising or carving a design with a hand-held graver or electric tool.

Epoxy. Two-component cement for adhering glass to glass or other materials.

Essence. A volatile liquid for thinning metallic paints.

Etching. Chemical or mechanical erosion of the surface to create a design.

Firebrick. A hard refractory brick with extremely high heat resistance; not to be confused with insulation brick sometimes used as a mold for firing glass.

Fired Paint. A finely ground glass enamel fired to specified temperature.

Flashed Stained Glass. Antique stained glass having a light-colored base with thin skins of deeper, richer, contrasting color. The contrasting color is removed with an etching or engraving method to create a design.

Flux. Colorless glass enamel ground to varying mesh sizes.

Fracture. Breaking, splitting, or cracking of glass.

Fracture Line. A score line made by a glass cutter or by a crack in the glass.

Fusing Glass. Combining glass pieces by melting them together.

Gilding. Applying gold, silver, or other metallic-colored paints; can be fired or unfired kinds.

Glass Cutter. A small hand-held tool with a tiny cutting wheel set in one end; used for scoring glass prior to separating it.

Grout. A creamy mortar filled in between glass pieces, ceramic tiles, and other mosaicked materials.

Grozing. Chipping away irregular projections to refine the cut edges of glass.

Incise. Cut.

Insulation Brick. A soft porous brick with high heat resistance; (not the same as firebrick).

Jewels. Small bits of colored glass that have been fired to round their edges.

Kiln. High-temperature oven with a refractory lining, used for firing glass, enamels, and ceramic clay.

Kiln Wash. A refractory powder made from equal parts of powdered kaolin and flint. Utilized in powdered or liquid form. Blended with water and brushed on kiln shelves and molds to shield them from sticking to glaze, enamel drippings, or fired glass. In powdered form, can be rubbed or sifted over molds as a separator.

Laminate. To unite by fusing materials between sheets of identical kinds of glass.

Liner. A brush with thin, flexible bristles designed expressly for making lines or stripes, but employed for designs as well.

Luster. A metallic overglaze paint.

Luster Essence. A luster thinner and brush cleaner for metallic paints.

Malleable. Easily shaped.

Mat, Matt, or Matte Finish. A dull, nonglossy finish.

Medallion. A flat decorative glass panel resembling a large ornamental medal, either painted, engraved, or embossed.

Metallic Lusters and Paints. Gilding paints in gold, silver, bronze, copper, brass, and other metallic colors.

Mold. A flat or contoured refractory base over which glass is fired, contoured, or slumped in the heat of a kiln.

Molecule. An elementary particle.

Negative Stencil. The stencil covering the area surrounding an open design.

Nonrepresentational. Without likeness; not representing any object; not realistic.

Opaque. Not transmitting light rays; impossible to see through.

Porous. Capable of absorbing liquids.

Positive Stencil. A stencil that covers the shape of the design itself so the area around it can be decorated (colored, etched, etc.). A pattern or template. See "Negative Stencil."

Pyrometer. An instrument that indicates kiln temperatures; usually attached to the kiln.

Rabbeted Frame. A frame with an offset groove cut around the edge to hold glass, mirror, or picture.

Refractory. Hard and resistant to high temperatures.

Reverse Painting. Painted pictures on the underside of flat or contoured glass, rendered in reverse, to create the desired image on the top or exposed side of the glass.

Score Line. A fracture line made by a glass cutter on glass prior to separation.

Scoring Glass. Making a scratched line with a steel cutting wheel set in a wood- or metal-handled tool, to effect a separation of the glass.

Seedy Glass. Glass having tiny bubbles that create a texture in it.

Separator. A protective powder, either sifted dry or brushed in solution with water, to which glass will not adhere.

Sgraffito. A decoration produced by scratching a design through a surface layer of unfired glaze, enamel, or paint to reveal a contrasting colored ground beneath it. The piece is then fired in a kiln.

Sheet Glass. Flat glass.

Single Strength. Window glass 1/16" thick.

Spar Varnish. Waterproof varnish.

Stress. Inner strain of glass caused by uneven heating or cooling, by fusing incompatible glasses together, or by fusing incompatible enamels to glass.

Template. A pattern cut from firm material to an exact shape as a guide in scoring glass shapes or stenciling decorative designs.

Translucent. Shining or glowing caused by diffused transmission of light rays.

Transmitted Light. Light that passes through transparent or translucent material.

Transparent. Having the property of transmitting light rays with clear vision of objects through the glass or liquid.

Turned Post. Shaped, rounded form achieved by application of a cutting tool on wood revolving in a lathe, such as a succession of rounded contours on a post or furniture leg.

Undercut. A cut that slants inward; prevents bent or cast glass from releasing from its mold.

Venting a Kiln. Leaving the door slightly ajar and/or a peephole open; this allows fumes to escape and slows heat rise.

Viscosity. The property of a fluid to resist internal flow which is increased as molten glass cools and thickens.

Volatile. Readily and quickly changed into vapor or gas.

Whiting. Calcium carbonate. A fine white powder used as a separator between glass and the surface on which it is fired to prevent them from sticking together in the heat of a kiln.

* Supply Sources

UNITED STATES AND CANADA
Check your local art, craft, hardware, and paint stores, and yellow pages
of the phone book. Write the following manufacturers for brochures and
names of nearest dealers.

Adhesives

(Epoxies, enameling gums)

Epoxy for Glass

Benesco Company
40 N. Rock Hill
St. Louis, Missouri 63119

H & M Plastics
129 S. Second Street
Philadelphia, Pennsylvania 19106

Thermoset Plastics, Inc.
5101 E. 65th Street
Indianapolis, Indiana 46220

Enameling Gum for Sifted Enamels

Thomas C. Thompson Company
1530 Old Deerfield Road
Highland Park, Illinois 60035

Liquid agar
Available at drugstores and
    ceramic suppliers

Enamels and Paints for Glass, Fired

Blythe Colours Ltd.
34 Brydon Drive
Rexdale, Ontario

B. F. Drakenfeld & Company
45 Park Place
New York, N.Y. 10007

L. Reusche & Company
2 Lister Avenue
Newark, New Jersey 07105

Standard Ceramic Supply
    Company
P.O. Box 4435
Pittsburgh, Pennsylvania 15205

Thomas C. Thompson Company
1530 Old Deerfield Road
Highland Park, Illinois 60035

Gilts and Lusters, Fired

Engelhard Minerals & Chemical
    Corporation
Hanovia Liquid Gold Dept.
1 W. Central Avenue
East Newark, New Jersey 07029

Thomas C. Thompson Company
1530 Old Deerfield Road
Highland Park, Illinois 60035

Paints and Gilt for Glass, Unfired

Fuller O'Brien Corp. (epoxy
    paints)
South San Francisco
California 94080
(Write for nearest dealer and
    color chart)

Mira-Plate Epoxy Paint
The O'Brien Corp.
South Bend, Indiana 46628

Spar varnish
Available at local retail paint
    stores

Tube oil paints (opaque and
    transparent)
Available at local artist suppliers

**Unfired Gilt, Gold, Silver, Metallic
Colors**

Connoisseur Studio, Inc. (Liquid
    Leaf)
P.O. Box 7187
Louisville, Kentucky 40207
(Write for nearest dealer and
    color chart)

**Glass: Stained Glass and Window
Glass**

Antique Stained Glass

S. A. Bendheim Company, Inc.

122 Hudson Street
New York, N.Y. 10013

The Blenko Glass Company
Milton
West Virginia 25541

Cathedral Stained Glass

Advance Glass Company
Newark, Ohio 43055

S. A. Bendheim Company, Inc.
122 Hudson Street
New York N.Y. 10013

Kokomo Opalescent Glass
    Company
P.O. Box 809
State and Market Streets
Kokomo, Indiana 46901

Window Glass and Plate

Libbey-Owens-Ford (LOF)
Pittsburgh Plate Glass Company
    (PPG)
(This glass available locally; check
    phone book).

Miscellaneous

Glass Cutters

The Fletcher-Terry Company
Spring Lane
Farmington, Connecticut 06032

Also available at hardware stores

**Medallions, Chains for Ornaments
and Medallions, Display Easels
(Wood and Plastic). Send for
Brochure**

Glass Masters Guild
621 Avenue of the Americas
New York, N.Y. 10011

General Supplies for Glass

S. A. Bendheim Company, Inc.
122 Hudson Street
New York, N.Y. 10013

Orange Craft Collective
213 King Avenue
Columbus, Ohio 43201

Whittemore-Durgin Glass
  Company
Box 2065 FA
Hanover, Mass. 02339

ENGLAND

Colorants

James Hetley & Company, Ltd
Beresford Avenue
Wembley, Middlesex

Johnson Matthey
Hatton Gardens
London EC 1

Wengers, Ltd
Stoke-on-Trent
Staffordshire

Unfired Colors

Tube oil paint and gilt available
  at artist suppliers

Glass

Claritude, Ltd
19 Dunraven Street
Park Lane
London W 1

James Hetley & Company, Ltd
Beresford Avenue
Wembley, Middlesex

Kilns

Catterson Smith, Ltd
Adam Bridge Works
Exhibition Ground
Wembley, Middlesex

Wild Barfield, Ltd
Elecfurn Works
Otterspool Way
Waterford By-pass, Hertfordshire

* Index